TMC Cl

1/8th 87

Common room and Dining Hall

h. Elevation.

MANSFIELD

PORTRAIT OF AN OXFORD COLLEGE

MANSFIELD

PORTRAIT OF AN OXFORD COLLEGE

Edited by **Stephen Blundell** and **Michael Freeden**
Photography by **Keiko Ikeuchi**

THIRD MILLENNIUM
PUBLISHING, LONDON

Mansfield: Portrait of an Oxford College

First published in 2012 by Third Millennium Publishing Limited,
a subsidiary of Third Millennium Information Limited.

2–5 Benjamin Street
London
United Kingdom
EC1M 5QL
www.tmiltd.com

ISBN: 978 1 906507 49 7

British Library Cataloguing in Publication Data
A CIP catalogue record for this book is available from the British Library.

Project Editor	Clare Howell
Design	Susan Pugsley
Additional photography	Katherine Blundell
Production	Bonnie Murray
Reprographics	Studio Fasoli, Verona, Italy
Printing	Gorenjski Tisk, Slovenia

Contents

Preface

Two Principals on Mansfield College

When this book was first envisaged in 2011 – the year of Mansfield's 125th anniversary – we little imagined what an outpouring of words, pictures and memories would follow. Articles were composed, the College archives were scoured, alumni wrote in and superb new photographs were taken. From each small item of fact or remembered pleasure, the pieces of the jigsaw have slowly come together and we can now behold, in its full glory, the portrait of a college that has meant so much to all of us who know and love it.

Whilst we need no book to convince us of Mansfield's special ethos, I invite you to let these pages evoke for you, once more, the spirit of camaraderie, of shared endeavour, of academic rigour and of social liberalism that imbue the very fabric of the College and its iconic building. This wonderful book will surely yield many fruitful hours of browsing and reminiscence and will be a lasting memento that alumni and staff – both past and present – will be proud to share with family and friends.

Dr Diana Walford CBE
Principal, 2002–11

It is a great privilege to be Principal of Mansfield College. The tradition of dissent, out of which this college grew, has been a dynamic force in our country. Dissenters have improved the way people live their lives today – without them we would not be living in a modern world. The intellectual tradition of dissent has been the wellspring of our liberty and our democracy. It played a crucial part in forging human rights and the rule of law. The stones of Mansfield College are steeped in this proud history. So, for me, its seductions were clear. Here was a place that had dared to be different in the midst of great tradition; a place that pursued excellence with as much vigour as any college, but which kept its gates open wide; a place that drew in students from across society, reflecting more accurately the world beyond Oxford. All in all, it was a place whose values I respected and where I felt I could make a contribution.

Like all successful institutions, Mansfield has evolved. It has shown itself capable of reinvention, moving from theological college to independent hall and then to a fully engaged Oxford college. The ethos of openness, egalitarianism and resistance to steep hierarchy has given rise to progressive policies, making Mansfield a warm and engaging community – a place where new ideas can be explored with intellectual rigour, where education is about more than a course of study, where every student is valued and where being 'the best we can be' is a goal with real meaning.

After 125 years Mansfield College has much to celebrate. But, as well as looking back and honouring all those who have contributed to its history, it is the perfect time to look forward and scan the horizon. It is the moment to scope our ambitions. The future presents many challenges and those who will lead our world tomorrow in every field of endeavour will have to draw on many skills. Mansfield's core strength is the very fact that it is different; its distinctiveness, its vitality and its values make its alumni perfectly suited to a changing social order.

So my tribute to Mansfield College on this special anniversary combines a salute to a proud past and a toast to an exciting future.

Baroness Helena Kennedy QC
Principal 2011–

PART 1

Origins and Reinvention

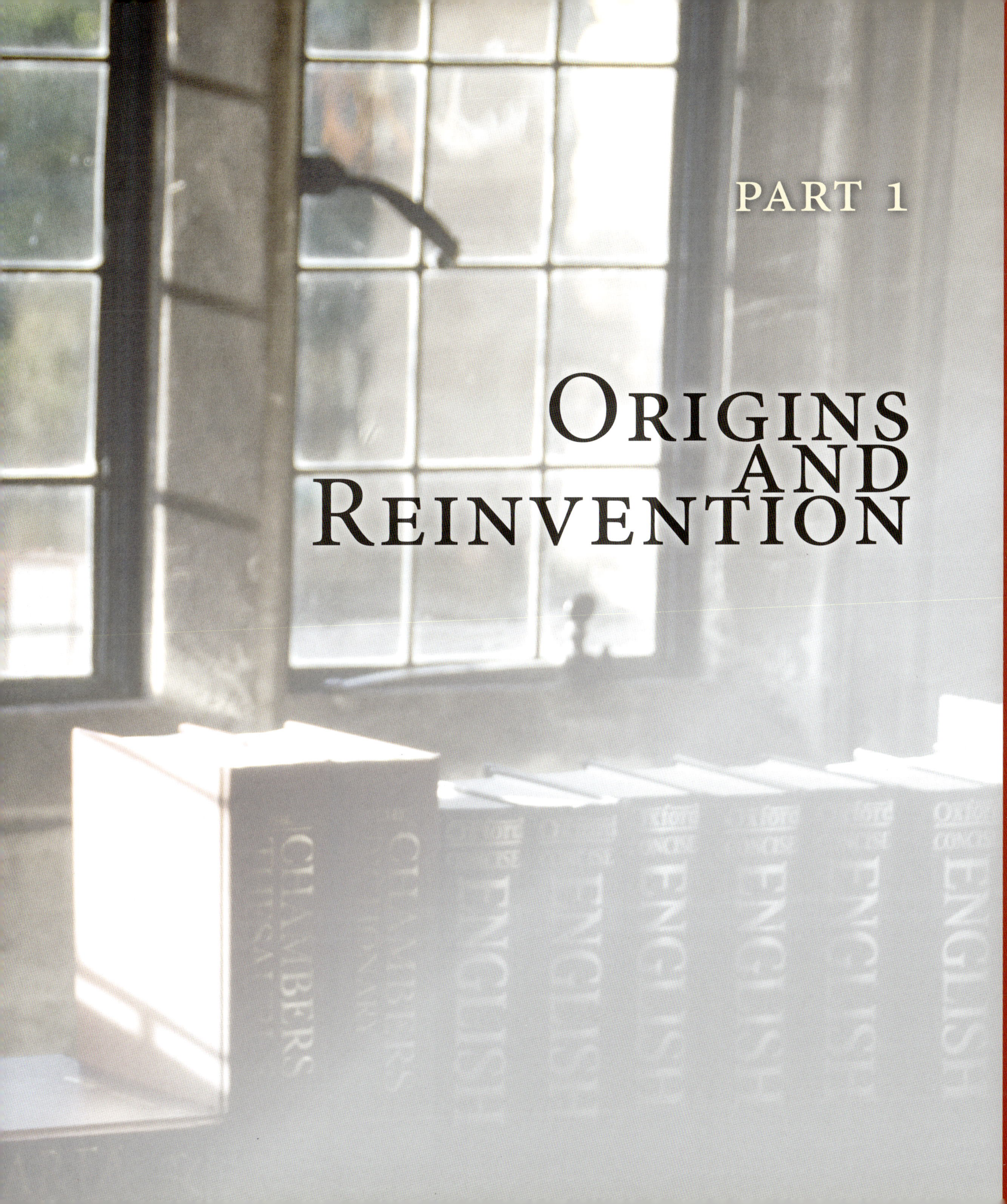

The Origins and Development of the College

Stephen Blundell

Through the centuries Oxford colleges have been founded by aristocrats, bishops, cardinals, monarchs and wealthy philanthropists. These institutions have undergone a slow evolution from their monastic foundations into modern secular colleges. Mansfield is therefore unusual for two reasons. First, its foundation is quite different. The existence of the College is not the result of a powerful individual's whim but rather of the need to fulfil a specific purpose: to bring the highest level of education to people who had been traditionally excluded from Oxford, an ideal to which Mansfield has stayed true. Second, it has undergone a far more rapid transformation into modernity from its original religious foundation than the vast majority of Oxford colleges. Founded firmly in the Dissenting tradition, Mansfield has perhaps found it easier than some to question assumptions about the status quo and to maintain a strong voice advocating educational change in Oxford, thereby facilitating its own evolution and fostering change in the wider University.

Previous pages: Bust of Dante in the College library.

Left: Group photograph taken at the opening ceremony of Mansfield College, April 1889.

William Gladstone endorsed the recommendations of the 1852 Royal Commission to reform Oxford and Cambridge Universities, which advocated the admission of non-collegiate students, and led to the dismantling of the Anglican monopoly.

Intriguingly, its buildings also shape its attitudes, the Victorian Gothic style echoing a medieval Oxford in which communities of scholars live and work together, bound by the ideals of scholarship. From its founding, Mansfield's aspirations have been to achieve academic excellence in its staff and students and to be a welcoming and friendly community of scholars. Despite all the changes in its relatively short history, Mansfield has instilled in its staff and students an unusual sense of loyalty and affection for the College and what it stands for. But the change has been considerable throughout the College's history, though perhaps this is unsurprising for an Oxford college that was born in the midst of institutional reform.

University Reform

In the middle of the 19th century the University of Oxford was overdue for a shake-up. It was something of a surprise that the man to do it was William Ewart Gladstone. Educated at Eton and Christ Church, a committed classicist (throughout his life he produced translations of various Latin authors as a form of relaxation) and a high Anglican, Gladstone was every inch a traditionalist. He nearly shipwrecked his own political career with his first book, *The State in its Relations with the Church*, which was published in 1838 while he was a minister in Robert Peel's government. Gladstone's lengthy prose made the case for the State to maintain and protect the interests of the Church of England (hardly then at any noticeable risk) more rigorously, and in particular he argued that Catholics and Nonconformists should be barred from holding government jobs. The more politically astute Peel withheld his backing from these inflammatory proposals, though he appreciated that they were a product of Gladstone's personal religious zeal. Thus it is quite extraordinary that in the early 1850s we find Gladstone, pillar of the establishment, intolerant campaigner against all forms of encroaching modernity and now Conservative Member of Parliament for the University of Oxford, at the forefront of advocating university reform.

In 1850 Gladstone had begun by bitterly opposing the setting up of a Royal Commission to examine the affairs of the Universities of Cambridge and Oxford, institutions that he held in the highest regard in their current state (though he was mainly interested in Oxford, and even there mainly Christ Church). But by the time the Commission reported its conclusions in 1852 he

The Gothic Revival building designed by Joseph James for Spring Hill College at Moseley, Birmingham. Founded as a seminary for the Congregational ministry in 1838, the rapidly expanding college moved to its new premises in 1857.

had become a convert, recognising that the Universities stood the best chance of preserving their distinctive traditions and clerical appointments by cooperating with some form of gentle reform. He helped to navigate the bill through the House of Commons, giving a bullish speech in its favour (despite having delivered his budget as Chancellor of the Exchequer only two days previously), and thus Gladstone played a part in the break-up of Oxford's Anglican monopoly. Now Dissenters could matriculate and proceed to bachelor degrees and, what was more, the Vice-Chancellor was empowered to open up private halls. This was really a compromise solution, and as Roy Jenkins has put it, the idea was to let 'the core colleges continue to be mostly the preserve of the rich, but let there be a periphery around them through which those of more modest means could get an Oxford degree and participate (to some extent) in the life of the university'.

In spite of ground gained in 1852, non-Anglicans were still barred from having any positions of responsibility in Oxford. They could not hold membership of Convocation since they were allowed to take only bachelor's but not master's degrees. They could therefore not become professors or Heads of House nor even hold fellowships or be members of governing bodies. Gladstone thought this situation was exactly as it should be and in

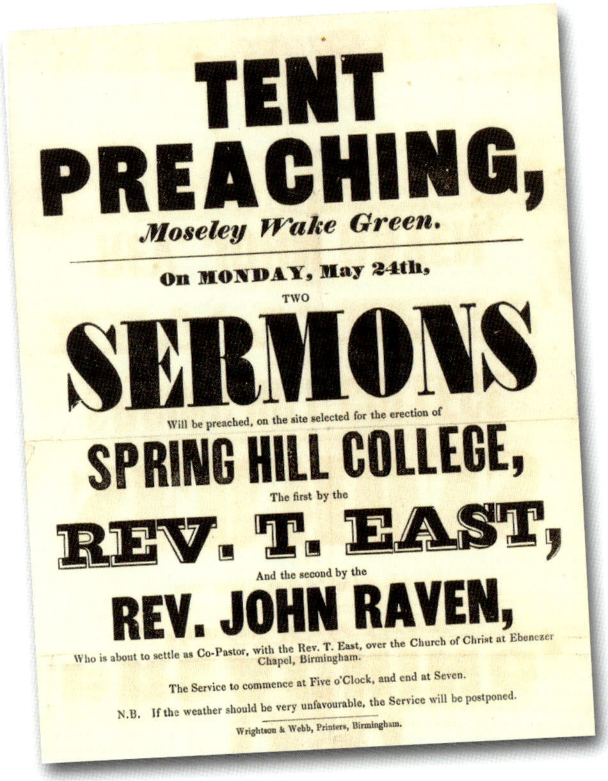

Left: A leaflet advertising two tent-preaching sermons on the new site chosen for Spring Hill College, Birmingham, in the early 1840s.

Below: The Whitehall Review, *26 October 1889, reacted unenthusiastically to the opening of Mansfield College.*

1870, now as prime minister, he strongly resisted the introduction of what was to become the University Test Act. Yet once again, gradually and with some reluctance, he became persuaded of the merits of the case. As he had done in 1852, Gladstone proceeded to swing round from intransigent opposition to full-blooded support, personally introducing the measure to the House of Commons in February 1871. From this date all academic appointments at Oxford, save those with a specific religious function, were open to those of all beliefs or none.

It seems that around 1871 Gladstone was discussing with leading Nonconformists the possibility of setting up a specifically Nonconformist college. 'Why don't you Nonconformists set up a college in Oxford?' he is recollected as having asked. Some in the Nonconformist tradition feared that Oxford's dreaming spires would spoil men 'from simple homes and simple surroundings' and make them too superior to be effective in ministering in the more modest environments of Congregational churches. Nevertheless, the idea took root, and it found fertile soil in Birmingham.

Establishing a Nonconformist College in Oxford

Spring Hill College was founded in Birmingham to train men for the Congregational ministry, and its existence was due to the generosity of the Mansfield family. George Mansfield lived nearby with his two sisters, Sarah and Elizabeth, although the family had originally come from Derby. In 1826 a trust deed for the new college they had funded was signed and provided for the Mansfield family to live on the estate but pay rent to the trustees. George Mansfield died in 1827, but his sister Sarah Glover (who had been widowed in 1821) took great interest in the new college, which finally opened its doors in 1838. Land was acquired on Moseley Common in 1840, and in 1857, following a vigorous

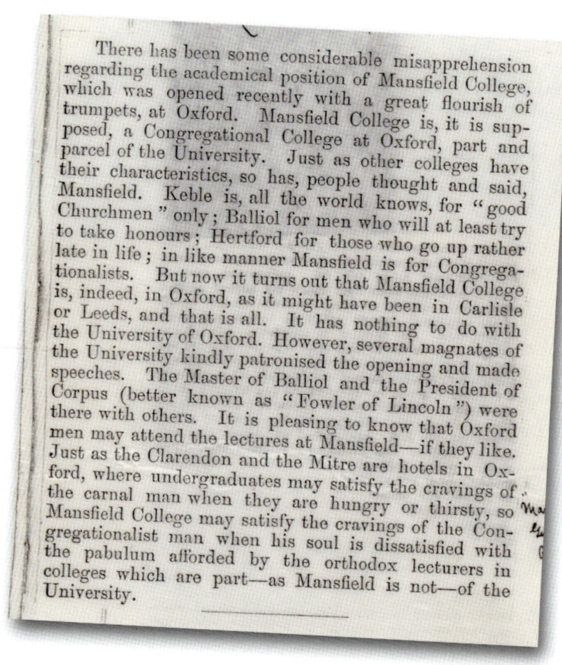

There has been some considerable misapprehension regarding the academical position of Mansfield College, which was opened recently with a great flourish of trumpets, at Oxford. Mansfield College is, it is supposed, a Congregational College at Oxford, part and parcel of the University. Just as other colleges have their characteristics, so has, people thought and said, Mansfield. Keble is, all the world knows, for "good Churchmen" only; Balliol for men who will at least try to take honours; Hertford for those who go up rather late in life; in like manner Mansfield is for Congregationalists. But now it turns out that Mansfield College is, indeed, in Oxford, as it might have been in Carlisle or Leeds, and that is all. It has nothing to do with the University of Oxford. However, several magnates of the University kindly patronised the opening and made speeches. The Master of Balliol and the President of Corpus (better known as "Fowler of Lincoln") were there with others. It is pleasing to know that Oxford men may attend the lectures at Mansfield—if they like. Just as the Clarendon and the Mitre are hotels in Oxford, where undergraduates may satisfy the cravings of the carnal man when they are hungry or thirsty, so Mansfield College may satisfy the cravings of the Congregationalist man when his soul is dissatisfied with the pabulum afforded by the orthodox lecturers in colleges which are part—as Mansfield is not—of the University.

Sarah Glover, the sister of George and Elizabeth Mansfield. Their generosity led to the founding of Spring Hill College.

Revd R.W. Dale, Congregational minister and former student of Spring Hill College, was a driving force in its transfer to Oxford and reconstitution as Mansfield College.

fundraising campaign, the college acquired an imposing new building, complete with a 78-ft tower and elaborately decorated library. The passing of the University Tests Act in Parliament, and Gladstone's suggestion that there should be a Dissenting college in Oxford, led the staff at Spring Hill to begin to discuss among themselves possible future opportunities for the college in one of the country's major universities. In 1883 the chairman of the College Board of Education, R.W. Dale, a former Spring Hill student himself, went as far as suggesting that Spring Hill College should relocate to Oxford or Cambridge. Dale was motivated by the idea that a healthy Christian community needs in it 'a fair number of men of great theological learning', and where better to train such people than at Oxbridge?

Oxford contained various individuals who were sympathetic to the opening of a Nonconformist college. The philosopher T.H. Green, a Fellow of Balliol, and the historian G.C. Brodrick, Warden of Merton, both liberal thinkers, were strong advocates. Benjamin Jowett, Master of Balliol (and Vice-Chancellor 1882–6), was another supporter, campaigning for 'a university and a college in which religion and rational enquiry did not conflict'. Thus Oxford was becoming more and more receptive to the idea of an institution like Spring Hill moving in.

Spring Hill formally decided to move to Oxford at a special meeting on 22 May 1884. On 17 May 1885 it was agreed that the name should be changed to Mansfield College in honour of 'the large-hearted family in whose Christian loyalty and zeal it had

Andrew Fairbairn, the eminent theologian, was the founding Principal of Mansfield College (1886–1909). A contemporary wrote, 'His talk was interesting from the width of his reading and the masterful vigour of his mind, but he had not much light play either in conversation or debate.' (From Mansfield College Caricatures 1906 *et seq. by W.H. Coats.)*

its origin'. In September 1885 it was also settled that each trustee and professor should make a declaration of Christian faith, as well as stating that 'he is a Dissenter from the Established Church'. At this point the theologian Andrew Martin Fairbairn consented to be Mansfield's first Principal, accepting an invitation that he had been given the previous March. (He had delayed his decision until all the negotiations had been completed and he was certain that the College would move to Oxford and nowhere else.) Fairbairn wanted Mansfield to be strictly a school, not a residential college. Its students should already hold degrees from Oxford, Cambridge or other universities but come to Mansfield to be prepared for the ministry.

The following month Dale, Fairbairn and other Mansfield representatives visited a site on Holywell Manor owned by Merton College, and by December they had agreed with Warden Brodrick's college to purchase the site for £3,000. An additional £300 was included in the package to cover the cost of building a road (now Mansfield Road) through the site that would join Holywell to South Parks Road. While the College buildings were being constructed, Mansfield College as an institution began its existence in temporary accommodation at 90 High Street (one room of which, by delicious irony, had been Charles I's headquarters during Oxford's siege in 1646). The first five Mansfield students commenced their studies in October 1886, each one of them enrolled as a non-resident graduate. Exeter College graciously elected Fairbairn to their Common Room, and he frequently dined there on Sunday evenings.

Meanwhile, two architects, both of whom had worked previously on projects in Oxford, were chosen to bid for the design of the buildings on the new site. Alfred Waterhouse's 'tired piece of French renaissance' lost out to Basil Champneys' 15th-century Gothic plan. Champneys' previous work included Newnham in Cambridge, Lady Margaret Hall in Oxford and, also in Oxford, the Indian Institute and the New College development in Holywell. His buildings at Mansfield were striking and impressive, providing three sides of a quadrangle, carved out of Taynton stone. The structure consisted of a central, south-facing gatehouse at the foot of a tower, flanked on one side by the hall and imposing chapel (unusually, north facing), and on the other by tutors' rooms, the library and the four-storey Principal's Lodgings. The final bill, including land, road, buildings, furnishings and gardens, came

The Champneys buildings under construction, c. *1888.*

to £48,733.0s.5d, a sum that was raised by 1892, only a few years after the formal opening in 1889. That grand celebratory event was attended by the great and the good from both the University and the Congregational Church, although Gladstone was a notable omission from the guest list – Dale had fallen out with him over Home Rule for Ireland. With a new building in place, the young College reorganised itself, replacing the 'Spring Hill Management Committee' with the new 'Mansfield Council' and thereby shedding some of its Birmingham representation.

One consequence of the building was that the dining room was relatively small, designed as it was for a couple of dozen students and their tutors, while the chapel was large and spacious, intended to accommodate a Nonconformist congregation drawn not only from Mansfield but also from the University and the city. This

A group of early Mansfield students, 1888.

A celebration lunch was laid on for the opening ceremony of Mansfield College in 1889.

imbalance in space would be a headache for the College in the future. Though there was initially additional space on Mansfield Road, the area slowly began to fill up. The Unitarians moved their Manchester College to Oxford in 1889, occupying for a period the vacated rooms on 90 High Street before their building was ready.

Fairbairn and his family occupied the Principal's Lodgings from 1889, and Fairbairn dined in College every weekday evening, often inviting notable guests. On 6 February 1890 Gladstone was the invitee. The former and future prime minister (he was then two years from commencing his fourth premiership) had spent a week at All Souls and, as a keen reader of Fairbairn's books, was glad to dine with the new Principal. The two men enjoyed an engrossing conversation on a subject of mutual interest: hymnology. Fairbairn (then 51 years old) walked the 80-year-old Gladstone back to All Souls at a rather late hour after the evening's proceedings had finished, but Gladstone (a prodigious walker into extreme old age) marched ahead at such a pace that the breathless Fairbairn could hardly keep up.

Fairbairn, a distinguished and renowned systematic theologian, set a high standard of intellectual rigour in the College. He was determined to equip his students with the intellectual tools they needed to understand modern critical developments in theology and emerge from Mansfield with a mature, thought-through Christian faith. Fairbairn could focus his energies on the students in what was then a small institution, with only about 25 students during the College's first years. All of the students were non-

William Boothby Selbie, celebrated orator and preacher, and the second Principal of Mansfield College (1909–32).

Nathaniel Micklem, third Principal of Mansfield (1932–53), and Professor of Dogmatic Theology, was a noted political activist during World War II.

residential and tended to be more mature than undergraduates at other colleges.

One of Mansfield's first students, James Vernon Bartlet, became a lecturer in Early Church History at the College and in 1900 became a professor. Nicknamed 'the last of the Early Fathers' and 'the elongated saint', Bartlet was extremely tall and scholarly, and his speech consisted of extraordinarily convoluted sentences. A keen tennis player, he would often invite his opponent to a quick knock-up with the words: 'Before we start the match proper, I will knock the ball to you, and you will knock the ball back to me, but, as it were, without contention.'

Fairbairn resigned as Principal in 1909, shortly after his 70th birthday, and he donated most of his library to the College. He died in 1912, and his funeral was held in the chapel. His successor was William Boothby Selbie, who had been educated at Manchester Grammar School, Brasenose and then, as one of the first five students, at Mansfield. Selbie was a superb orator; in the words of Nathaniel Micklem, one of his students and his successor as Principal, 'the pulpit was his throne'. He could hold an audience in the palm of his hand, and Mansfield became the place to come and hear fine preaching on a Sunday morning. The chapel was frequently packed so that it was not unknown for people to be turned away when Selbie was in the pulpit.

During this time Mansfield retained its high reputation for scholarship through the work of its tutors, particularly G.B. Gray (Professor of Hebrew and Old Testament Exegesis) and

C.H. Dodd, Professor of New Testament Greek and Exegesis from 1915–29, and one of the most significant 20th-century theologians.

George Buchanan Gray, 'a very popular tutor' and Professor of Hebrew and Old Testament Exegesis. (From Mansfield College Caricatures 1906 *by W.H. Coats.)*

C.H. Dodd (Yates Professor of New Testament Greek and Exegesis). Dodd, the advocate of 'realised eschatology', was one of the most significant theologians of the 20th century. It was a great loss to the College when he moved to Manchester in 1929 to take up a chair in biblical criticism, but he frequently returned to lecture at Mansfield, the last time in 1971, when, aged 87, he delivered an address at a summer school.

Oxford had long been a male institution, but the first women's colleges were founded at the end of the 1870s, and some of the University's new female students attended Mansfield's chapel services. In 1904 the JCR agreed to allow 'ladies' to play tennis on the College courts at certain times, though the vote was not unanimous. Constance Todd came up to Oxford in 1908 to read History at Somerville and convinced Selbie both that she was an academically suitable candidate for admission to Mansfield and that she had a genuine calling to the ordained ministry. She was not technically a graduate, despite qualifying for a good honours degree (women were not yet permitted to be awarded their degrees), but Selbie admitted her to the College, and in 1917 she became the first woman ordained to the ministry, in a mainstream trinitarian Christian denomination, in Britain. Four more female students were admitted to Mansfield during Selbie's principalship (which ended in 1932), more of a trickle than a flood, but the precedent had at least been set.

More progress was to come. In 1913 the University agreed that candidates for the degree of Bachelor of Divinity (BD) or Doctor of Divinity (DD) were no longer required to be in holy orders of the Church of England. Selbie was given a DD by decree in 1920,

Constance Mary Todd, the first woman to be ordained to the ministry, in a mainstream Christian denomination, in Britain, and her husband, fellow Mansfield student, Claud Coltman, on their wedding day, 18 September 1917.

becoming the first Nonconformist to receive one since 1662. It was the end of a long struggle for Nonconformists to gain acceptance into the higher echelons of Oxford's theological establishment. Mansfield continued to be very much on the map in terms of academic developments in theology, and important thinkers in this field came to the College. Albert Schweitzer visited Mansfield in 1922 to give the Dale Memorial Lecture (which he delivered in French), and Karl Barth dined in Mansfield with Principal Micklem in 1938 while he was in Oxford to receive a DD.

Although the academic life was healthy, there were clouds on the horizon. The number of Congregational churches continued to increase until 1908, but the population in Britain was increasing more quickly. After 1908 the number of churches, the number of members and the number of ministers all started a slow and inexorable decline. This began to affect the College in two ways. It slowed down the number of ministerial candidates, which dropped further during the First World War, plummeting to just two in 1918. Numbers temporarily recovered as soldiers returned from the war, but soon fell off again. This reduction in the number of candidates had an obvious effect on the College's finances.

As storm clouds gathered once more over Europe, Mansfield was to find itself connected to the coming conflict in various ways through its links with Germany. Adam von Trott came to Mansfield as a visiting student from Germany in Hilary Term 1929, returning to Oxford in 1931 as a Rhodes Scholar at Balliol. Von Trott was put to death in 1944 for his part in a plot to assassinate Hitler. In the 1930s the new Principal, Nathaniel Micklem, had been one of the few Christian leaders who had tried to understand how the rise of Hitler in Germany was going to affect Europe. Micklem had himself studied in Germany and visited the country in 1937 and 1938, seeing at first hand how the Church there was being persecuted. He participated in an officially illegal ordination ceremony and attended various clandestine activities of the Confessing Church (the Protestant church that arose to oppose government attempts to Nazify the official German Protestant church) and reported back on his experience to friends in Britain, including Cosmo Lang, the Archbishop of Canterbury. He recalled later: 'I have never felt evil as a physical, almost tangible, thing as I did on that visit to Berlin.' He felt that the Nazi regime was 'the negation of God erected into a system of government' and warned that an integral element of National Socialism was 'a ferocious and illimitable anti-Semitism'. In 1939 he published *National Socialism and the Roman Catholic Church*, copies of which were smuggled into Germany in false

Mansfield quadrangle and porters' lodge, c.1950.

PRINTED FOR PRIVATE CIRCULATION ONLY.

No. 137 JULY. 1950.

MANSFIELD COLLEGE MAGAZINE

DEUS LOCUTUS EST NOBIS IN FILIO

CONTENTS

Editorial ... 21
Malcolm Spencer ... 21
Griffithes Wheeler Thatcher (1865-1950) 23
Memories and Meditations ... 25
Book Reviews:—
Wesley: A Man with a Concern ... 27
Psychology and Mental Health ... 28
Morality and God ... 30
Communism and Christian Faith ... 31
Book Reviews (continued):—
The Church and Music ... 32
The Growth of the Old Testament ... 33
The Biblical Doctrine of Election ... 33
The Jews from Cyrus to Herod ... 35
Put in Your Hand ... 37
To the Brethren of the Dispersion ... 37
J.C.R. Notes ... 40
The Old Men's Meetings 1950 ... 41
Alia ... 42

dust wrappers. Mansfield's buildings were requisitioned during the war, but when the College got its buildings back, and celebrated its Diamond Jubilee in 1946, there was a new challenge to face.

Mansfield's ongoing financial crisis was reaching a critical stage. Income was declining year on year as subscriptions from individuals and donations from churches started to dry up, and for the first time expenditure was starting to outstrip income. The buildings were beginning to need serious attention, but nothing had ever been set aside for structural repairs. What was more, the College was beginning to consider the merits of becoming residential, requiring more buildings to be built on the College's site, for which, of course, there was absolutely no money. A still more radical idea was brewing: that Mansfield should become a

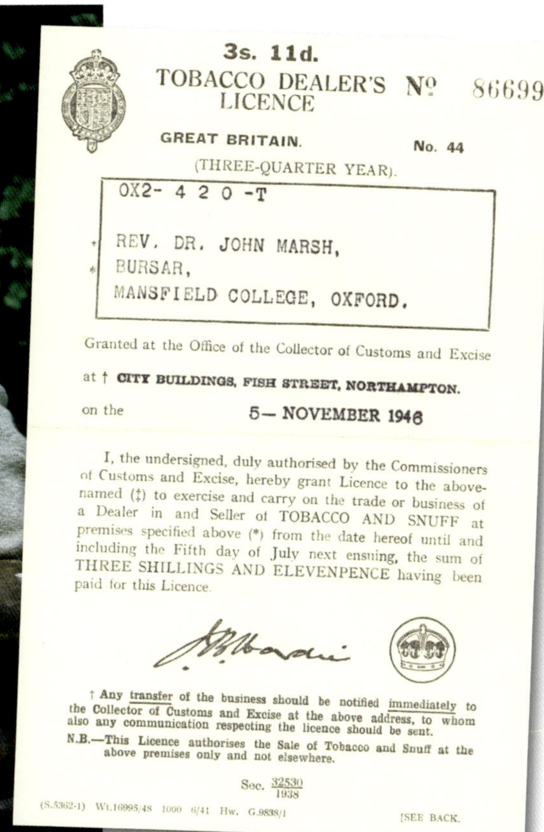

3s. 11d.

TOBACCO DEALER'S LICENCE Nº 86699

GREAT BRITAIN. No. 44

(THREE-QUARTER YEAR).

OX2- 4 2 0 -T

REV. DR. JOHN MARSH,
BURSAR,
MANSFIELD COLLEGE, OXFORD.

Granted at the Office of the Collector of Customs and Excise

at † CITY BUILDINGS, FISH STREET, NORTHAMPTON.

on the 5— NOVEMBER 1946

I, the undersigned, duly authorised by the Commissioners of Customs and Excise, hereby grant Licence to the above-named (‡) to exercise and carry on the trade or business of a Dealer in and Seller of TOBACCO AND SNUFF at premises specified above (*) from the date hereof until and including the Fifth day of July next ensuing, the sum of THREE SHILLINGS AND ELEVENPENCE having been paid for this Licence.

† Any transfer of the business should be notified immediately to the Collector of Customs and Excise at the above address, to whom also any communication respecting the licence should be sent.

N.B.—This Licence authorises the Sale of Tobacco and Snuff at the above premises only and not elsewhere.

Sec. 32530/1938

(S.5362-1) Wt.16995/48 1000 6/41 Hw. G.9838/1 [SEE BACK.

Far left: John Marsh, fourth Principal of Mansfield (1953–70). Under his guidance, Mansfield was established as a permanent private hall (PPH) in 1955, and expanded to include the teaching of a wide range of non-theological subjects.

Left: One of the Principal's more unusual jobs was to obtain a licence to sell tobacco from HM Customs and Excise.

hall of the University and build up an undergraduate population of up to around 200 students. These were all grand dreams for the future, but the financial crisis motivated the contemplation of far less palatable options to save money, including a merger with another Free Church college in Cambridge or an amalgamation of theological colleges in Oxford.

The new Principal, John Marsh, went to see the University registrar in 1954 and explained Mansfield's dilemma. He was listened to sympathetically, but disappointingly was told that no funds from the University Grants Committee could be made available before 1960 at the earliest. However, the registrar pointed out that if Mansfield became a permanent private hall (PPH) – a status made possible following a 1918 University statute and taken up at that point only by Campion Hall (Jesuit) and St Benet's Hall (Benedictine) – then its students would become eligible for local authority grants, widening the supply of students and removing the need for the College to supplement grants.

The College moved rapidly on this suggestion, submitting its application to the Hebdomadal Council. The case made was pretty solid, since the College was able to tick the relevant boxes: Mansfield had a proper constitution recognised by the Charity Commissioners; it was not run for profit (rather the reverse!); its Principal was a graduate of the University; and the College was located well within a two-and-a-half-mile radius of Carfax (outside which PPHs were not permitted to exist). Anxious to seal the deal, the College even offered to change its name to 'Mansfield Hall', if that would help oil the wheels, but stated that it preferred to keep the name by which it had been known since its founding.

Hebdomadal Council gave its blessing to the College's request and agreed to not ask for a name change. Hence in 1955 Mansfield College became a PPH of the University of Oxford.

With its newly acquired status, the College proudly began to assume the trappings of a member of the club. Its coat of arms, adopted in 1886, had never been officially registered, and it was now necessary to do this. Unfortunately, the coat of arms had already been bagged in 1563 by one Lancelot Manfeld of Skirpenbek, Yorkshire, and could not be used. John Marsh therefore set about commissioning a replacement coat of arms, and the result was confirmed by the College of Arms. Mansfield now had something to put in the Oxford University Calendar, in which it was now permitted to have an entry.

A far more important change followed. Financial viability required more students, but though the supply of students wishing to study theology was small, there were many more who wanted to study non-theological subjects. Universities were expanding in the 1950s, and student numbers were increasing everywhere, so there was a large market to tap into if Mansfield could diversify its subject base. This meant appointing some non-theological tutors (the first joined in 1960), as well as asking Fellows of other colleges to accept responsibility for teaching certain subjects. One such imported tutor was the biochemist Arthur Peacocke, then a tutor at St Peter's, who taught chemistry at Mansfield. Peacocke had done important work on the structure of DNA and later became well known as an original thinker in the fields of science and theology, and the importance of the dialogue between the two.

Reform was in the air in other ways. Mansfield ordinands had not been permitted to marry during their studies, but this rule was relaxed in 1959, prompting a rush of engagements that earned the College the appellation 'Romancefield'.

PPH status had a negative side effect for women. This occurred because Mansfield had joined a university that had, by rule, no co-educational colleges. They were all-male or all-female. The College that had educated Constance Todd in 1913 had now to specify that one female student who studied from 1955 to 1958, entering just as PPH status was adopted, was no longer formally a member of the JCR and could use it only until lunchtime, except by express permission of the JCR president. Anxious not to cause ructions in a university to which they had only recently been admitted, Mansfield therefore resisted becoming officially co-educational until it became recognised University policy, which finally occurred in 1979. The College nevertheless continued to admit women for ordination training, although the status of these female ordinands remained somewhat irregular. The first female undergraduates arrived in Mansfield in 1979, although, of course, women had been admitted to theological courses since 1913, even

Main image: The old lodge and grounds, c.1960. The obelisk brought from Spring Hill College can be seen under the trees in the top left-hand corner.

Above: The old lodge: Donald Sykes (before he became Principal) talking to a passing student, c.1960.

The Principal, John Marsh, with the Queen Mother at the opening of the new building in 1962; it was formally named the John Marsh Building in 1993.

'Orthodox and pious, he preached eloquently – usually of sin and forgiveness. He sang loudly and forcefully, and always out of tune … He inspired love and respect and some fear in his students, probably in equal measure, but his loyalty to all of us and to the College and to the denomination and to his Lord was unending.'

About John Marsh
Graham Stephenson – *1967, Ordinand*

if in rather small numbers. The first female member of the SCR was Pamela Busby, lecturer in English, who joined in 1971. She was closely followed by Janet Dyson, lecturer in mathematics in 1977. The College slowly but surely became less of a male bastion.

More students meant new accommodation on site was needed. (PPHs were bound by University rules not to have more than five undergraduates living out of college, although the rule was waived for Mansfield for several years to give the College time to adapt.) The College launched an appeal in 1959 to raise £160,000 for the new buildings and increase the tutorial endowment fund. Marsh told the subscribers: 'It is either this or the extinction of Mansfield.'

Building work began at the end of 1960. The old lodge was demolished, and the new structure of Guiting stone from the Cotswolds filled out the south side of Mansfield's quadrangle. Opened in 1962 by the Queen Mother, paid for only in 1968 (the appeal had raised only a third of its target by 1962), the new building acquired a formal name – the John Marsh Building – only in 1993. It provided accommodation, a new lodge and two tutors' houses along Mansfield Road. The two houses were occupied initially by George Caird and family and Donald and Marta Sykes, but they have now become sets of tutors' rooms with student accommodation on the top floors.

The College was now teaching across a much wider subject base and embarked on a road that would eventually lead to full college status in 1995 – the process of change continuing in a series of small but steady advances. In 1972 the United Reformed

The celebration tea after the opening of the new building, 1962.

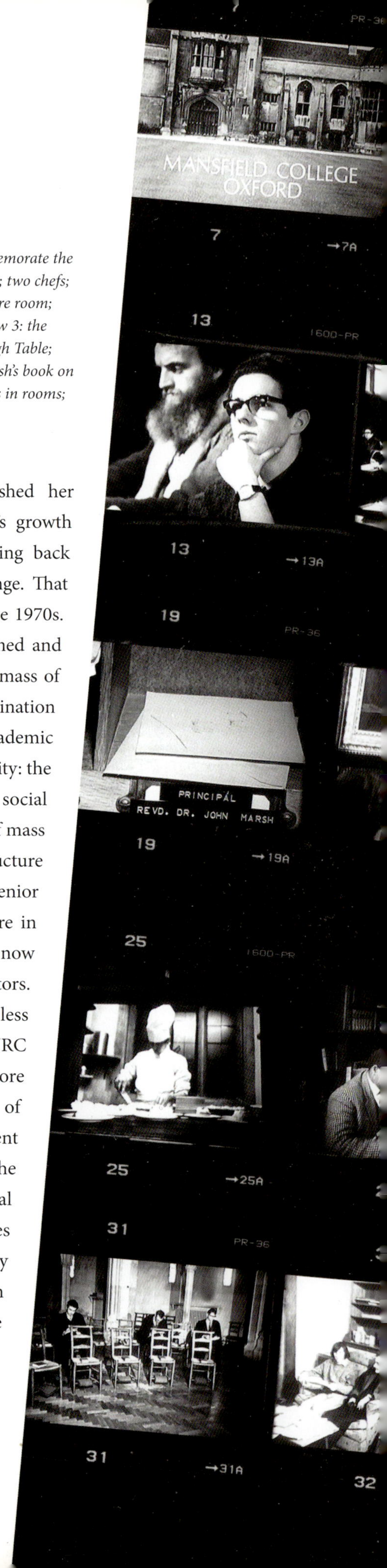

Stills from a documentary film made in 1969 by Peter Armstrong (1966, Theology) to commemorate the retirement of John Marsh. From left to right: Row 1: John Marsh in his study; going to chapel; two chefs; John Marsh with an ordinand; papers and mortar board. Row 2: students listening; the lecture room; John Marsh and Nathaniel Micklem; student asleep; an ordinand; view from the kitchen. Row 3: the Principal's mail box; chaplain Charles Brock; aerial view of the College; student relaxing; High Table; Broad Street. Row 4: chef; in the library; John Marsh and Nathaniel Micklem looking at Marsh's book on St John; rowing; coach and megaphone; outside staircase. Row 5: ordinands in class; students in rooms; dinner in Hall; Whigmore's Dairy; Wally Buckingham, College steward.

The Principal's Lodgings.

Church (URC) was formed, bringing together the Congregational and Presbyterian Churches. This brought Mansfield's ordination training programme into a potentially wider market, but it introduced tensions between the wishes of the new Church and Mansfield's emphasis on the primacy of academic excellence and, in particular, the College's now resolute policy to treat its non-theological education as of equal value to its theological education.

In 1996 Elaine Kaye published her meticulous history of Mansfield's growth towards full college status, looking back over a century of continual change. That change markedly intensified in the 1970s. As Mansfield's subject base widened and its fellowship grew, the centre of mass of the College swung away from ordination training and towards the major academic disciplines pursued in the University: the humanities, the sciences and the social sciences. This shift in the centre of mass had a profound effect on the structure of Mansfield. From 1970 the senior members of the College who were in charge of particular subjects were now designated Fellows, rather than tutors.

Inevitably the College became less wrapped up with the affairs of the URC and began to interact more and more strongly across the departments of Oxford University. The appointment of Michael Freeden in 1978 was the first the College made in official collaboration with representatives from the appropriate University faculty. Mansfield was now well on its way to full integration into the wider University.

The Reinvention of the College

Michael Freeden

Although a renewed drive towards fundamental change at Mansfield began in the 1960s, the past 40 years have seen it undergo an accelerated transformation, the likes of which have not been experienced by any other Oxford college during the same period. One way of symbolising that is to recall the old Gestetner wax stencil-based duplicating machine – already in the 1970s a technological antique – and to observe today's super-slick photocopiers and laser printers. But the story of Mansfield's nigh-revolutionary mutation is far more intricate than the evolution of its electronic infrastructure. What has remained constant is its liberal, open and egalitarian spirit; almost everything else is unrecognisable – not least its aura of professionalism and self-confidence – as it has moved dramatically out of the shadows of Oxford academic life.

Above all, Mansfield has re-engaged with its tradition of dissent and tolerance by applying it to a new, more secular age. The Nonconformist spirit has remained, but the psychology has been overhauled. The College has reinvented itself over the past

Helen Lacey, Tutor in Late Medieval History, giving a tutorial in the Tower Room.

Students deep in discussion (left) and (below) signing up for societies at a freshers' event in the JCR.

40 years, forging its own destiny with considerable conviction and unexpected courage.

What has the College not experienced in recent decades? A gastronomic revolution, with soups of the highest standard; an 18-year-old financial genius, Guy Hands, who opened an Oxford art shop within a year of arriving as an undergraduate; the filming location of eight minutes of *Heaven's Gate*, one of Hollywood's most infamous fiascos, yet one that brought the College much needed cash; a centenary ball (1986) with dancing until dawn; involvement (by association) with the famous Oxford Boat Race mutiny of 1987 through its club president, Mansfield man Donald Macdonald; a radical and contentious rebranding exercise by a notable PR firm; the sojourn of the 39th former President of the United States in the Principal's Lodgings; incursions by animal rights activists who mistakenly assumed that the College was connected to a research laboratory across the street; and a fraudster who appropriated Mansfield letterheads to sell abroad a fake Mansfield MSc diploma (Oxford colleges are not permitted to confer degrees). Underlying or accompanying all these was a spirit of reform, of adventure, of ingenuity, of determination and of radical thinking, together with a gradual shedding of organisational dilettantism.

An Academic Overview

In the 1960s it was still not uncommon to refer en bloc to 'the non-theological subjects' studied in College. In 2009 we saw the final vestiges of the ministerial training that was once the pride of Mansfield ended by an unsustainable drop in potential ordinands. The exponential growth of the 'non-theological subjects' illustrates a remarkable shift in the centres of academic, social and cultural gravity of the College. As an academic subject, theology had to take its place alongside other, larger, fields of study, as English, geography, history, PPE (philosophy, politics and economics) and law raced ahead, particularly from the 1970s.

Concurrently, the chapel – not only a building imbued with the ongoing spirituality of Mansfield but also a site of great

Chaplain Charles Brock with Justine Wyatt, assistant chaplain and the first Oxford woman college chaplain, after a service of thanksgiving for the refurbishment of the chapel in 1985.

architectural and artistic significance, as John Muddiman notes on page 69 – has adapted to those changes and recalibrated its position. Initially, that meant being placed by forward-looking chaplains and performers at the core of burgeoning musical events, both sacred and less so. Instrumental in that development – in both senses – was Carolyn Brock, who directed Mansfield music and served as its organist for many years. Carolyn was the wife of Charles Brock, a colourful and liberal chaplain, who epitomised the atmosphere of change in his spiritual generosity and mischievous sense of humour. The ease of passage of the College into a new relationship with its religious origins was due in no small part to his vision. Recently, Mansfield's musical activities have expanded from the dominance of the chapel organ and choirs to embrace a rich variety of lunchtime recitals and other concerts under the current chaplain, Tanya Rasmussen, and director of music, John Oxlade; and there have even been plays and occasional opera and ballet performances. The chapel has diversified further by becoming a venue for freshers' dinners and other social events, while maintaining its primary role as a centre of worship for some members of the College. We hope that the figures gazing down from the windows acquiesce and that some even approve.

The secularisation of Mansfield saw it first focusing on the humanities (oriental studies was added in the early 1990s, initially under Ron Nettler and then Alison Salvesen) and the social sciences. The advent of mathematics in 1977, however – bridging the categories of science and logic – was followed from the late 1980s by the permanent addition of physics, engineering and materials as academic subjects with their full Fellows, while human sciences joined as a smaller subject, first under Joy Boyce and then Andrew Gosler. PPE eventually acquired an economics Fellow (Antoni Chawluk) and more gradually two Fellows in philosophy (Katherine Morris and Paul Lodge) to assuage Michael Freeden's previous solitude as sole PPE Fellow.

Secularisation meant more than just the reorganising of an academic palette, however. The opening of the College gates – dismantled for scrap metal during the Second World War and reinstalled in the mid-1980s together with a set of railings to rescue the College from honourable mention in the Good Thieves' Guide to Oxford – to increasing numbers of students of all religions, and none, contributed significantly to transforming the ideological and social character of Mansfield. As the light breezes of modernity began to waft through Oxford University, the long overdue (re)-inclusion of women in 1979 was another step in the direction of secularisation. For notwithstanding the achievements of the United Reformed Church in that area, women have not been at the heart of the vocational, as distinct from the practising, side of the major religions, and relatively few have of late applied to Mansfield for its religious attributes. The dynamics of male

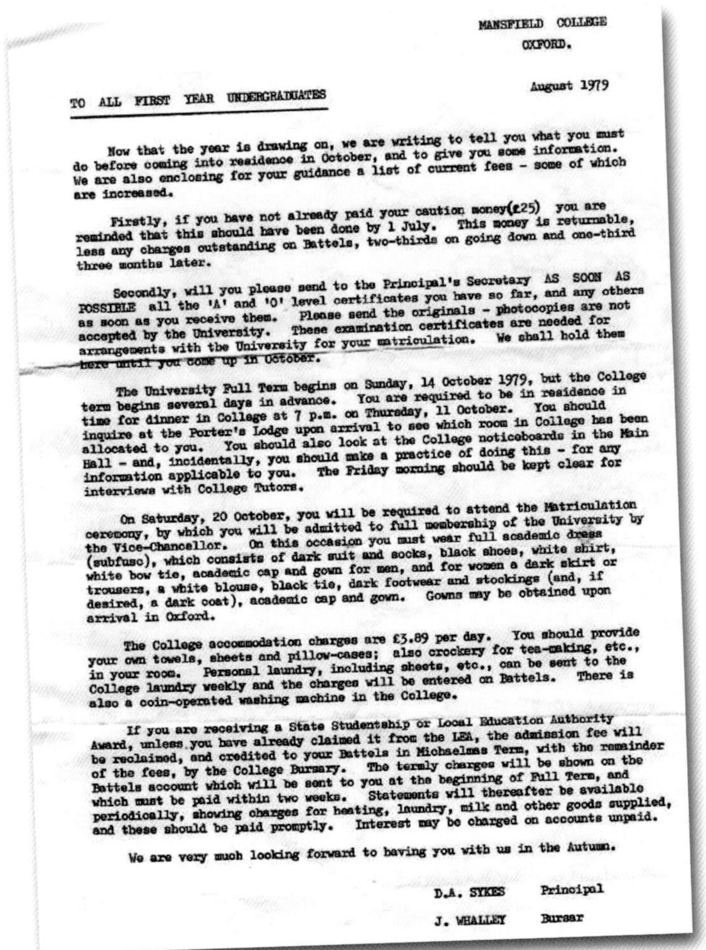

MANSFIELD COLLEGE
OXFORD.

August 1979

TO ALL FIRST YEAR UNDERGRADUATES

Now that the year is drawing on, we are writing to tell you what you must do before coming into residence in October, and to give you some information. We are also enclosing for your guidance a list of current fees - some of which are increased.

Firstly, if you have not already paid your caution money(£25) you are reminded that this should have been done by 1 July. This money is returnable, less any charges outstanding on Battels, two-thirds on going down and one-third three months later.

Secondly, will you please send to the Principal's Secretary AS SOON AS POSSIBLE all the 'A' and 'O' level certificates you have so far, and any others as soon as you receive them. Please send the originals - photocopies are not accepted by the University. These examination certificates are needed for arrangements with the University for your matriculation. We shall hold them here until you come up in October.

The University Full Term begins on Sunday, 14 October 1979, but the College term begins several days in advance. You are required to be in residence in time for dinner in College at 7 p.m. on Thursday, 11 October. You should inquire at the Porter's Lodge upon arrival to see which room in College has been allocated to you. You should also look at the College noticeboards in the Main Hall - and, incidentally, you should make a practice of doing this - for any information applicable to you. The Friday morning should be kept clear for interviews with College Tutors.

On Saturday, 20 October, you will be required to attend the Matriculation ceremony, by which you will be admitted to full membership of the University by the Vice-Chancellor. On this occasion you must wear full academic dress (subfusc), which consists of dark suit and socks, black shoes, white shirt, white bow tie, academic cap and gown for men, and for women a dark skirt or trousers, a white blouse, black tie, dark footwear and stockings (and, if desired, a dark coat), academic cap and gown. Gowns may be obtained upon arrival in Oxford.

The College accommodation charges are £3.89 per day. You should provide your own towels, sheets and pillow-cases; also crockery for tea-making, etc., in your room. Personal laundry, including sheets, etc., can be sent to the College laundry weekly and the charges will be entered on Battels. There is also a coin-operated washing machine in the College.

If you are receiving a State Studentship or Local Education Authority Award, unless you have already claimed it from the LEA, the admission fee will be reclaimed, and credited to your Battels in Michaelmas Term, with the remainder of the fees, by the College Bursary. The termly charges will be shown on the Battels account which will be sent to you at the beginning of Full Term, and which must be paid within two weeks. Statements will thereafter be available periodically, showing charges for heating, laundry, milk and other goods supplied, and these should be paid promptly. Interest may be charged on accounts unpaid.

We are very much looking forward to having you with us in the Autumn.

D.A. SYKES Principal
J. WHALLEY Bursar

Notice sent to the new intake of undergraduates in 1979.

Right: Some of the Oxford college shields, as per 1886, painted on the SCR ceiling. In the top right-hand corner is Oxford City's coat of arms, which has an ox crossing a ford.

and female proximity further propelled the College into one of modernity's features and has resulted in the occasional marriage between Mansfield students over the years. On the senior side, women had served as College tutors well before 1979, but the first woman Fellow, Kate Flint, was elected only in 1986, since when that number has increased to 12 at the time of writing. And of course, Mansfield crossed another Rubicon by appointing Diana Walford and then Helena Kennedy as its latest Principals.

From the 1960s onwards Mansfield's ambition to become a full member of the community of Oxford colleges was being increasingly voiced inside its walls, but the marginalised status of permanent private halls (PPHs) made that difficult – the Franks Report on the role of Oxford in higher education did not even mention the PPHs, despite Mansfield's submission. Instructively, that ambition had been painted on Mansfield's ceilings since its founding: the hall and the SCR were decorated with all the shields of the Oxford colleges as per 1886, with the addition of Cambridge University's and Oxford City's coats of arms, as if to say: 'By hook or by crook, we shall get there!' Even in the 1970s Mansfield approached that goal slowly and gingerly, its early brazenness forgotten, all too often looking over its shoulder at the practices of other colleges rather than embarking on its own distinctive route, as it later did. It was clear that internal reform was to be a prerequisite to full college status. Few, however, would have imagined that the task would be so arduous and drawn out and that so many stages would be necessary.

The first major move in that direction was the drawing up of a College constitution. Under its final chair, the amiable Lord Bancroft, the College Council – a body that had gradually and informally ceded decision-making on most College academic and administrative matters to the SCR – was replaced in 1987 by a Charity Commissioners' Scheme. This stipulated a body of trustees, including the Principal and College Fellows as well as representatives of the United Reformed Church and the Congregational Federation, while the Principal and Fellows of Mansfield constituted the Governing Body (the detailed story can be found in Tony Lemon's account; see pages 93–9). Standard Oxford nomenclature was now anticipating the College's keen desire to become a full college and to signal to the University and the other colleges that Mansfield's time had come.

A year later, Mansfield's inclusion in the colleges admissions system meant that it was now able to compete on equal footing for the best student candidates. The days when Mansfield had to struggle over obtaining first-choice applicants, relying instead to a considerable extent on the overflow from other colleges, its tutors laboriously sifting through second- and third-choice applications in the dead of winter in unheated depositories dotted around Oxford, were beginning to recede. And the image of the College as a mainly theological institute, initially hard to shed and detrimental to attracting a wide range of candidates, was becoming obsolete. What cannot be underestimated in that process was the strong emotional attachment that Mansfield elicited from its Fellows, who were dedicated in countless supererogatory ways to 'institution-building' but also genuinely and often passionately involved in the nurturing of its hopes and objectives, usually steeped in revisionist conversation over College lunches or engulfed in the mundanities of its daily life. That pleasure was frequently accompanied by overwork and exhaustion in a college that had little administrative back-up – if, say, tutors needed to send something by registered post, they would have to walk to town themselves and queue at the post office at the cost of 45 minutes of valuable time.

Alongside those developments the secular academic reputation of the College was rising fast. English, through a succession of Fellows from John Creaser through Kate Flint, Ros Ballaster and Lucinda Rumsey, was not only producing impressive results in the final honour school but, no less importantly, was

Michael Freeden, Emeritus Professorial Fellow in Politics, in his study, 2011.

home to internationally acclaimed researchers. Awards of jointly funded College and University posts to John Creaser, Tony Lemon (geography) and then Michael Freeden (politics) were early signs of recognition, as were, over the years, major national research awards to Michael Freeden and later to Ros Ballaster and Kathryn Gleadle (history). The scientists, including Janet Dyson (mathematics), Norman Booth, Stephen Blundell and Steve Biller (physics), John Harding and Chris Martin (engineering), and John Sykes and Jason Smith (materials science), were making important advances in their respective fields, and major national research grants were coming their way as well. Ian Sargent (reproductive science), Marcel Fafchamps (development economics) and Jon Chapman (applied mathematics) were further appointments for which the University secured – and Mansfield welcomed – an attachment.

Fellows were also increasingly involved in departmental and University administration. Undoubtedly, Mansfield's place in the University sun was crucially aided by the augmented Oxford, national and international reputation of its Fellows' research findings and publications: they had become the sine qua non for full membership of a university whose gold-standard status was universally known and admired. From the mid-1990s onwards a growing number of Fellows obtained professorships or readerships in the University Recognition of Distinction exercises. The College was also able to secure a steady flow of junior research

George Caird, fifth Principal of Mansfield (1970–7). A renowned New Testament scholar, he 'lectured as he preached, almost without a note', Henry Chadwick observed.

fellowships (JRFs), particularly in the sciences. As for theology as an academic subject, it was far from lagging behind, opening up to new approaches and remaining at the cutting edge with Joel Rasmussen joining John Muddiman as a Fellow in theology. All that was steadily coming to the attention of applicants, not least in the growing number of graduate students the College managed to attract in research and taught courses. And a notable proportion of undergraduates was arriving from the European mainland, east and south Asia, and the United States.

A further number of recent appointments – Jocelyn Bell Burnell (astrophysics), James Marrow (energy materials), Michèle Mendelssohn (English), Derek McCormack and Richard Powell (geography), Pavlos Eleftheriadis and Nancy Eisenhauer (law), Marina Galano (materials science), David Leopold (politics) and Helen Margetts (society and the internet) – have reinforced the quality of the fellowship and diversified its range.

The Principals

In parallel, a new breed of Principal emerged. Following George Caird (1970–7), a distinguished theologian who had resigned to accept a chair in New Testament studies, Donald Sykes became the College's first lay Principal (1977–86), and the warmth of his personality and open and collaborative style led Mansfield into new, democratic pastures. A short, two-year, pre-agreed interim with Jan Womer as Principal (1986–8) followed Donald Sykes's early retirement as a consequence of ill health. It then took a while to search for a new Principal, and for the first time the College used professional head-hunters to ensure a high-quality field. The choice fell on Dennis Trevelyan, a top-ranking civil servant who was Mansfield's first Principal to have no personal link with the theological traditions of the College. The three Principals that have followed him all arrived with distinguished public service records in their wake: David Marquand (Principal 1996–2002), Mansfield's first non-theological academic, had an eminent career in UK and European social democratic politics and was a political historian and journalist; Diana Walford (Principal 2002–11), the first scientist to head Mansfield, was a foremost civil servant in the field of health; and Helena Kennedy (Principal from 2011) is a leading human rights and civil liberties lawyer and a Labour member of the House of Lords. It was, however, under Dennis Trevelyan's leadership that the College finally attained its holy grail: full collegiate status.

The array of publications by Fellows of Mansfield reflects the wide range of their interests and disciplines.

A Long Process

Shortly before Trevelyan's appointment the College had begun to negotiate with the University. In fact, no sooner had the 1987 constitution been adopted than Mansfield had to negotiate a new route of legal and administrative restructuring. Mike Mahony, the history tutor whose untimely death in 1994 deprived Mansfield of one of its most committed members, was at the time Acting Principal, and almost immediately (in 1988) opened negotiations with the University about the terms for becoming a full college. By 1989 an agreement in principle had been secured from the Hebdomadal Council, but it set an unrealistically high bar of £5.5 million endowment as a condition for that desired status. Fortunately for anxious Mansfield fundraisers, the proviso was rescinded four years later.

In the meantime, after protracted negotiations with the Charity Commissioners, with the religious denominations that had

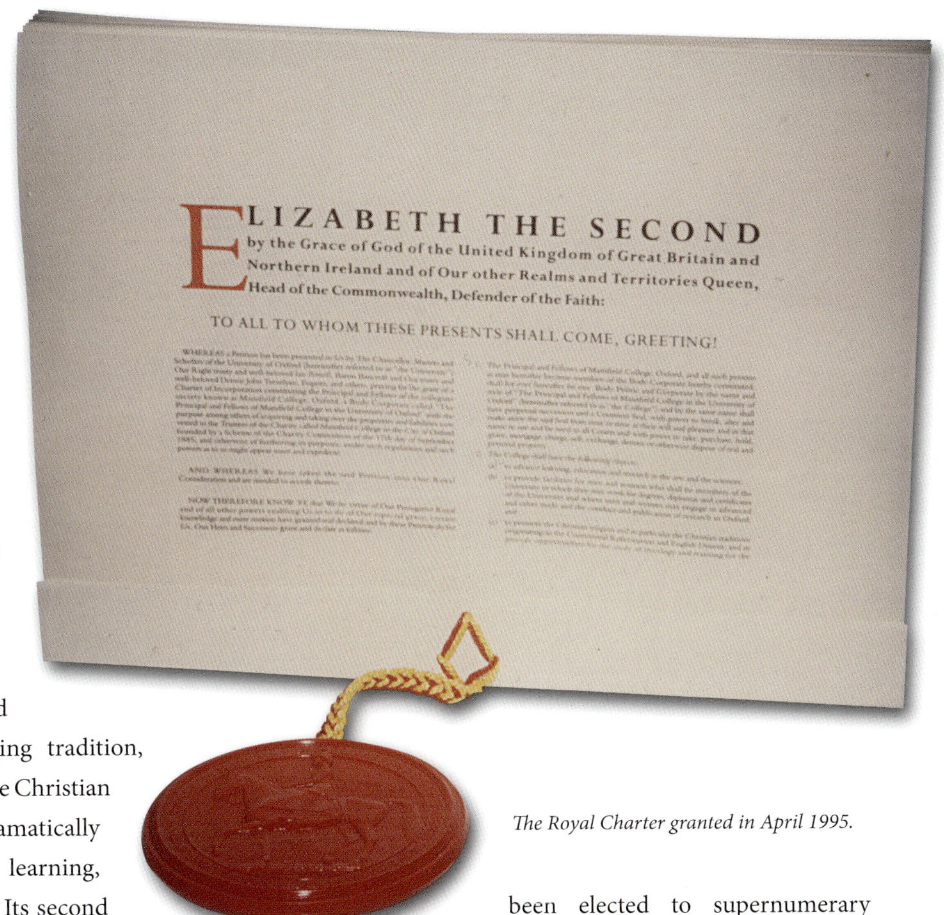

The Royal Charter granted in April 1995.

founded Mansfield and with the Privy Council, a Royal Charter, combined with the Statutes of Mansfield College, was granted on 11 April 1995. It was approved by The Queen on 31 May 1995, at which point Mansfield finally attained full collegiate status. Dennis Trevelyan travelled to London and returned by bus with that mighty document tucked under his arm in a brown paper parcel. Perhaps that was fittingly significant, being entirely in line with the unstuffiness bordering on informality that has characterised Mansfield's persona in recent decades and has endeared it to its junior and senior members.

The Royal Charter enshrined the inherited Christian role of the College in the Dissenting tradition, including the study of theology and training for the Christian ministry, but the College's first object now dramatically emphasised its educational role: 'to advance learning, education and research in the arts and sciences'. Its second object became the provision of facilities for men and women to study for degrees of the University and to engage in advanced study and research. The Governing Body replaced the trustees as Mansfield's supreme decision-making body, thus sanctioning de jure what had already become de facto. A large College celebration in June acknowledged the end of one journey and the accelerated continuation of another.

Due to Mansfield's small size it has always relied on a body of non-permanent stipendiary lecturers to complete the delivery of its teaching obligations. Over the years some of them have been elected to supernumerary fellowships in recognition of the quality of their scholarship and the unusually heavy duties they have been prepared to adopt, including the holding of major College offices. Recently the College office of Senior Tutor, the person co-ordinating the academic policy of the College, has been held by some of those College Fellows – Michael Freeman (geography), Philip Kennedy (theology) and now, on a permanent basis, Lucinda Rumsey – while the expanding role of Tutor for Graduates is now being held by another College Fellow, Helen Lacey (history). Their crucial contributions have also

The Women's 1st VIII, 2011.

been acknowledged through including stipendiary lecturers in those sections of Governing Body meetings from which they are not constitutionally barred, and in doing so Mansfield has been one of the leaders across the University. Mansfield has benefited enormously from that practice of democratic inclusion, which has strengthened its participatory and egalitarian ethos.

At the heart of Mansfield are its students, undergraduates and graduates, whose raison d'être the College is. A lively, intelligent, variegated and shifting population, now numbering about 220 undergraduates and 50 graduates, each year group leaves its mark in countless ways in addition to studying and obtaining University and College prizes and awards – student journalism, sports (in particular rowing), drama (public and private), debating societies, the occasional rent strike and charitable activities.

Student activities: a JCR meeting and a dance in the chapel.

One such example is the Mansfield settlement in London's East End. Following an Oxford tradition dating back to the late 19th century, when Oxford students spent time and energy among underprivileged youths, the link was restored in the 1990s, also including visits of London schoolchildren to Mansfield.

In 2000 Mansfield drove forward a major initiative: an outreach programme designed to attract state school students who would not normally consider applying to Oxford. Aware

Right: Students at Mansfield House, 1897. The Mansfield University House Settlement was one of several University settlements that opened in deprived areas of the East End of London in the 1880s. It was intended to give students first-hand experience of living and working within a poor community.

of the low proportion of state school applicants to Oxbridge, Mansfield launched the Access for Excellence campaign and led a consortium of Oxford colleges in an attempt to focus on the further education sector. The campaign was spearheaded by David Marquand, Janet Dyson and Lucinda Rumsey (the latter two consecutively occupying the post of Tutor for Admissions) and not least by Mansfield's specifically appointed recruitment officers, Janine Fisher and Helen Etty. The account of that initiative, which attracted both funding and international recognition, appears on pages 101–7. It was entirely in harmony with Mansfield's insistence on dismantling some psychological barriers to application and was driven by the appreciation that talent was spread equally across the country. That talent had to be tapped into – not only to offer individuals opportunities where such had been lacking, but also for the good of Oxford University itself, which needed to benefit from the best minds wherever they were to be found. The number of state school students at Mansfield has increased considerably, and it is now leading Oxbridge colleges on that front.

The new pressures on College resources, internal and external, highlighted the central importance of the Mansfield Development Office, formed in the later 1980s as more and more colleges sought to supplement their income from private sources in an increasingly harsh climate for British universities. The Development Office has since then been the focus of countless campaigns, some inevitably more successful than others, but on the whole a hub of tremendous initiative and resourcefulness. Gaudies, telethons, parents' evenings and alumni reunions in the United States have become part of the social landscape of the

The Mansfield Settlement's first home was two houses in Barking Road in Newham.

*Left: The Chancellor, Lord Jenkins of Hillhead, planting a handkerchief tree (*Davidia involucrata*) at the opening ceremony of the Hands Building in 1993, with (from left to right) Duncan Forbes, bursar, Principal Dennis Trevelyan, Carol Trevelyan, Lord Bancroft and Robin McGarry, College steward.*

Below: Guy Hands, the financier and Mansfield PPE alumnus, through whose generosity the new student residential accommodation was built.

College. Major refurbishment of the College took place in the late 1980s. A new residential building for students, constructed through the generosity of Guy Hands, was opened behind the John Marsh Building in 1993. Guy also financed a new research programme on dyslexia, as well as playing a crucial role in the external Development Board; he has additionally set up the annual Hands Lecture, to be given by high-profile speakers from the fields of politics and public policy. In 2006 the Garden Building was opened, financed in part by Kanto Gakuin University in Yokohama, Japan, and by the Ebara Corporation in Tokyo, Japan. It provides not only student accommodation but also seminar rooms and facilities for visiting Japanese researchers and, during vacations, accommodation for the many external conferences that significantly supplement Mansfield's income. The conferences themselves necessitate a separate administrative arm of the College with its own operations manager, currently Lynne Quiggin. At the time of writing, plans are advanced for two buildings designed by Rick Mather Architects, who have just won international recognition with the recently extended Ashmolean Museum in Oxford. Masterminding all that is the augmented role of the bursar as the chief administrative officer of the College. As that crucially important post has evolved, so has its integration

New buildings as envisioned by Rick Mather Architects.

into SCR and College life more generally through the geniality of its most recent occupants, Duncan Forbes and Steve Waterman.

Among Guy Hands' more unusual initiatives was to hire Bell Pottinger Consultants in 1999 to engage in a rebranding exercise of the College. Following extensive interviews across various Mansfield populations, the consultants came up with a list of values associated with Mansfield: tolerant, dedicated, informal, friendly, risk-taking, radical, inclusive, innovative and caring. If that *embarras de richesses* was not enough, Mansfield was also assigned a concoction of personality traits: warm, confident, sceptical, welcoming, receptive, committed, happy, proud and hungry (the last no reflection on our dedicated kitchen staff). The coup of the exercise was a redesigning of the College letterhead with a logo described as 'forward-looking, dynamic and challenging' and consisting of a series of black and yellow dots

The Garden Building was opened in 2006.

floating onwards and upwards, partially cupped by a faint outline of the old shield. Most members of the SCR accepted that change with indifference, some even regarding it as an improvement on the traditionalism of the existing letterhead, though one senior member refused to have any truck with that stationery revolution and hoarded as many of the older sheets as he could find. The logo was quietly laid to rest some six years later, but the College was secretly amused with the assortment of compliments – mostly self-bestowed!

In the rapid growth of any institution there are some failures. In 1992 the College embarked on a major departure in its own structure by setting up a research centre under its auspices, the Oxford Centre for the Environment, Ethics and Society (OCEES), whose brief it was to explore human responsibility towards the non-human natural world. The idea was to combine an area close to the ethico-religious sensibilities of the Dissenting tradition with Mansfield's newer strengths in philosophy, politics, economics and law and to fill a gap in the burgeoning Oxford development of environmental studies, hitherto more scientific than human value-oriented. Researchers were recruited in anthropology, economics and law, and a post was funded by the International Fund for Animal Welfare. At first, the momentum of the centre was considerable, spawning conferences and an impressive published series of occasional papers, and, following a period of internal management, an expert on water policy, Neil Summerton, was appointed as director from 1997 to 2002. But OCEES ran into dual difficulties. Despite strenuous efforts it proved impossible to raise sufficient funds to make it a viable institution; at the same time the University was powering ahead on so many environmental fronts that OCEES was simply overtaken. Its researchers found jobs elsewhere and it was allowed to lapse. Mansfield had learned that it was sometimes necessary to rein in its ambitions.

Alma Jenner joined Mansfield in 1976 and presided over the College library and its expansion for 35 years.

The College library is not only an architectural gem but has itself undergone changes instituted by Alma Jenner after joining librarian Gordon Trowell in 1976, who later retired. Despite being saddled with a cumbersome classification system, Alma introduced automation in 1997, and the library expanded to take over neighbouring rooms, which included dispensing with a prized snooker table, while culling some of its older books and journals – for which there had been little demand – to make way for a rapidly

Long-serving and loyal College scout, Susan Keane has worked at Mansfield for 30 years and has a College room named in her honour.

Wally Buckingham was a stalwart presence in College for three decades, serving as College steward, boat-club coach, and keeper of the wine cellar even after his retirement in 1977.

expanding collection. Even before that culling, a thief had reduced the Mansfield collection by 200 volumes in one fell swoop. Since then Mansfield's openness has had to be slightly curtailed, and library security has been tightened. In line with the inflation in national monitoring practices, cameras lovingly follow people around the College. Alma also performed wonders with developing a College archive, as well as spearheading the refurnishing, and refurbishing, of the library, abetted by a grant from Oxford University Press and a generous gift from Charles Brock.

The changes in the range and breadth of Mansfield's 'official' profile also embraced many other remarkable features. Mansfield is justly famed for its port of entry, the lodge, and for the benevolence, eccentricity and sheer humanity of its porters. First impressions in a student's or visitor's life are vitally important, and as the initial public relations arm of the College, some of its colourful characters – in recent years Mike Sherwood, Hugh Flint, Barry Mawby and Terry Greenwood – have held the fabric of the College together in countless ways, as Duncan Forbes's piece tellingly illustrates (see pages 64–7).

The kitchen – under the guidance of Lynn Partridge and her talented team – has undergone the kind of culinary metamorphosis that befits the gradual internationalisation of the south of England's palate in recent decades. A variety of hot meals and cold salads, no longer drained of taste or stocked with fat

'Although many colleges boast about having the best food, after eating meals at several colleges I have to say that nothing compares to Mansfield cooking. The food at Mansfield is real home-cooked, comfort food, and simply delicious! The chefs always go out of their way to experiment and come up with wonderfully satisfying meals. It was always a delight to go for a meal in College, surrounded by the warm and cozy atmosphere of our beautiful hall. And the desserts always surprised and exceeded expectations. Mansfield food is pure pleasure!'

JULIA SCHAEFER GOMEZ – *2010–11, MSc in Nature, Society and Environmental Policy*

Lynn Partridge, Food & Beverage Manager.

Dining in Hall: students and Fellows together.

and excess calories as was the wont of Oxford institutional meals until the 1980s, has enhanced the reputation of Mansfield's cuisine across the University. The Mansfield College magazine recorded in 1987 that: 'At a College guest night there recently it was pleasing to notice that the guests took the evening's menu away with them.' Above all, Mansfield's soups are essays in inventive taste, texture and colour (see A Soupçon of Mansfield, page 158).

Two American Presidents (technically ex-Presidents, but their title is retained for life) have trod on Mansfield ground. In 2001 Bill Clinton inaugurated the Rothermere American Institute (RAI), a fine modern building adjacent to Mansfield, and attended a large celebration in a marquee on the College's lawn. Mansfield

Opposite: Hard at work in the kitchen.

President Bill Clinton inaugurated the Rothermere American Institute, built on part of Mansfield's grounds, in 2001.

ceded a strip of land to the University in order to enable the RAI's construction and was adequately compensated by a contribution to its endowment. Various links between College and RAI were forged, and its director is a member of the SCR. In 2007 that experience of Presidential presence was surpassed when Jimmy Carter, in Oxford to receive an Honorary Doctorate from the University, spent three days in the Principal's Lodgings with his wife Rosalynn Carter, delivered the annual Hands Lecture, was guest of honour at a College dinner, and was elected an Honorary Fellow of Mansfield.

There is another side to studying at Mansfield. In the 1960s a North American summer school was instituted for American

President Jimmy Carter, in Oxford to receive an Honorary Doctorate in 2007, with the Principal, Diana Walford. He was also elected an Honorary Fellow of Mansfield.

The United Kingdom is experiencing a period of tightening and retrenchment across the higher educational sector. Mansfield cannot escape from that, but it is academically, financially and, above all, mentally better equipped than ever to meet those challenges. Its innovative spirit and radicalism have enabled it to negotiate through troubled waters in recent decades and to emerge stronger and more assured of its distinctiveness. It owes much to the prescience of its founders, though even those blessed with the most foresight would have been challenged to dream up such a transformation. Above all, Mansfield College has established a convincing record of fashioning its own destiny that will continue unabated as it navigates its way through the 21st century.

ministers. From the 1980s Mansfield began to host programmes mainly for American undergraduates to enjoy a junior year abroad. Those were sufficiently successful for the College to organise its own programme in 1990 and to justify the appointment of directors who combined a JRF with running, and recruiting for, those courses, now known as the visiting student programme. Accommodation requirements were partly met by constructing a small building on Cowley Road. Those associate students, usually some 35 a year, while following tailor-made study plans, have played their part in undergraduate life and have been a mainstay of Mansfield support in their College afterlife.

The President and his wife punting with the Principal and Arthur Walford.

Mansfield at War

Alma Jenner

Long before the government requisitioned the buildings in 1939, clandestine activity, led by the Principal, Nathaniel Micklem, was already stirring within the College. On a visit to Germany in 1937 he witnessed the work of the illegal and persecuted Confessing Church, had meetings with leading German churchmen, including Dietrich Bonhoeffer, and brought back pamphlets and literature printed by the underground press.

Left: Adam von Trott, visiting student in 1929, was put to death in 1944 for plotting the assassination of Hitler.

Below: Alec Whitehouse, a theology student, accompanied the Principal on his visit to Germany in 1937.

Principal Nathaniel Micklem (centre, front row) twice visited Germany in 1937 to meet members of the Confessing Church. In 1938, he also sent the chaplain, John Marsh, (seated to Micklem's left) on a covert mission to Berlin to deliver a letter and secret papers to them.

'Nat's' friendship with the Dominicans in Oxford enabled him to stay in Catholic monastic communities during a second visit to Germany in 1937, when he was accompanied by one of his students, Alec Whitehouse, who made further contacts with the Confessing Church. These were dangerous liaisons, and elaborate procedures needed to be in place before private conversations could begin. The chaplain, John Marsh, was despatched on a covert mission to Berlin in 1938 by Micklem to deliver a letter to members of the Confessing Church. This and various secret papers were stitched into J.M.'s surgical corset by his wife Gladys. It is not surprising that the Mansfield Common Rooms during the war years included a young German pastor, Hans Kramm, a former Prussian supreme court judge, Herbert Hirschwald, and a classical scholar, Dr Gunther Zuntz, all refugees from the Nazi regime.

Hedin Bronner, US army, at work in one of the government huts at nearby Harris Manchester College.

Canadian chaplains used Mansfield's JCR and ante-chapel for services during the summer, c.1941.

Government huts and outbuildings soon sprang up around Oxford after the College was requisitioned. Along Mansfield Road at Harris Manchester College, the Geological Unit took root near the School of Geography, while at Mansfield, where the main building was guarded day and night, windows were bricked up at the side of the long corridor and an air-raid shelter was built behind it. Only the chapel, the library and the Principal's Lodgings remained for College use. Micklem wrote: 'If you peeped in the front door you would see a vast erection of sandbags stretching from floor to ceiling … and the library can only be entered (and that by the slim) by means of the private staircase from my lavatory. A temporary JCR rigged up in my basement enjoys an electric fire, a few pictures, some JCR furniture and a wonderful smell of sandbags.' There was 'open house' in the Lodgings on Saturday evenings, when the Principal read poetry and Erik Routley and Peter Scott provided musical entertainment. The chapel (where the future prime minister Harold Wilson was married in 1940) was used for lectures and morning service, while a new kitchen garden was created by digging up the Principal's private tennis court.

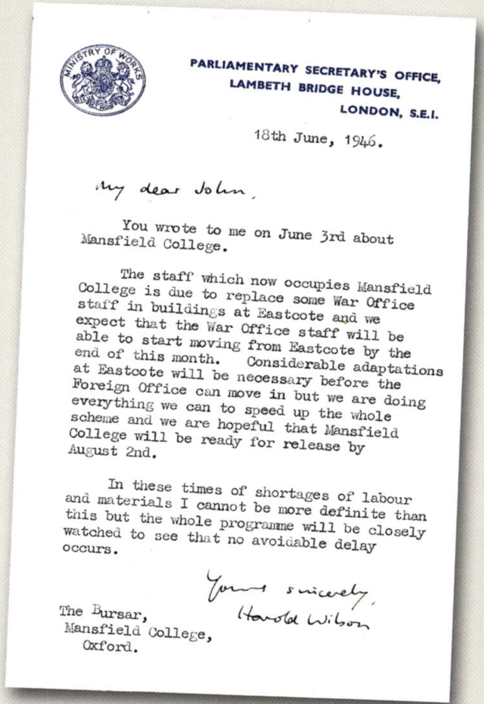

MINISTRY OF WORKS

PARLIAMENTARY SECRETARY'S OFFICE,
LAMBETH BRIDGE HOUSE,
LONDON, S.E.I.

18th June, 1946.

My dear John,

You wrote to me on June 3rd about Mansfield College.

The staff which now occupies Mansfield College is due to replace some War Office staff in buildings at Eastcote and we expect that the War Office staff will be able to start moving from Eastcote by the end of this month. Considerable adaptations at Eastcote will be necessary before the Foreign Office can move in but we are doing everything we can to speed up the whole scheme and we are hopeful that Mansfield College will be ready for release by August 2nd.

In these times of shortages of labour and materials I cannot be more definite than this but the whole programme will be closely watched to see that no avoidable delay occurs.

Yours sincerely,
Harold Wilson

The Bursar,
Mansfield College,
Oxford.

Letter from Harold Wilson in 1946 confirming the transfer back to Mansfield of its requisitioned buildings.

In 1942 the codes and ciphers branch of the Foreign Office requisitioned the library: 40 staff transferred from Bletchley Park to Mansfield to prepare British code books and re-enciphering tables, while active-service personnel received training. Code books and other materials were sent to be bound at the nearby Oxford University Press. The Admiralty took over the rest of the buildings for further secret work.

It was not until 1946 that the College regained its buildings. A letter from Harold Wilson, then at the Ministry of Works, to John Marsh confirming the transfer marked the end of another chapter in Mansfield's history.

Mansfield in the Movies: *Heaven's Gate*

Tom Lancaster

The 1980 western film *Heaven's Gate* has a bad reputation: a film so bad that it destroyed the director's career, so expensive it drove United Artists into bankruptcy, a production so poorly organised that after the first five days of filming it was four days behind schedule, and a film so absurd that it includes a five-minute fiddle solo played by a man on roller-skates. The film's opening scene is set in Harvard in 1870 but couldn't be shot in Harvard because of a ban on filming there. Much of it was shot in Mansfield.

Mansfield was transformed for the filming of Heaven's Gate.

Alma Jenner featured as an extra in the film.

The eight minutes of *Heaven's Gate* that feature Mansfield were filmed in one week, with a disruptive set-up beforehand. Transforming 1979 Mansfield into 1870s Harvard involved constructing a papier mâché façade to create an entrance arch and cover the new parts of the College building. Most dramatically, it also involved the erection of an enormous tree in the quad, around which the celebrating Harvard students were to dance. The tree had been bought in Cirencester for a small fortune and cut into pieces for transportation. It was reconstructed in the quad by slotting numbered branches into the trunk and gluing painted leaves into the branches (and the marks made by the base of the tree construction on the lawn are still visible from the right angle).

The 90-ft beech tree, implanted in the quad, required a crane to manoeuvre it into position.

'The filming of part of Heaven's Gate *took place while I was in my first year. Probably the most remarkable thing about the filming was the amount of preparation and effort that went into it compared with the length of time in the final film, just the first few minutes.*

A large tree was selected, cut down and delivered to the College. We watched it arrive on the back of a lorry. It was so big that it was impossible to manoeuvre the lorry into the College, so a crane was used to raise the back of the lorry while the driver reversed it over a small wall.'

JOHN LYSONS – *1979, MATHEMATICS*

Rehearsals of the dance scene involved a Strauss waltz being played at deafening volume for the best part of a day. Mansfield students were recruited as extras and, in some cases, were recruited by the actor John Hurt to pop into town and buy bottles of whisky. Mansfield's Lutheran theology Fellow, Merlyn Satrom, had planned to take some photographs of the production but was initially prevented from entering the College as the production crew couldn't believe that an American was an Oxford academic rather than a tourist.

Although the film was a financial catastrophe, Mansfield's finances benefited enormously. The meeting to decide the College's fee was scheduled to start at midday for one hour, followed by lunch. It was still going on at 3.00 pm with no lunch having been eaten and resulted in the fellowship demanding more than double the initial offer. When the production resulted in damage to the Tower Room, the College succeeded in getting United Artists to pay for its decoration, which was masterminded by Carol Mahony, the wife of the history Fellow, who also featured as an extra in the film.

The story for Mansfield could easily have ended in disaster: a scene involving lit candles in the windows of the library was approved by the then bursar on the grounds that 'we have insurance'!

Heaven's Gate was panned by critics on its release, but afterwards began slowly to win praise as a masterpiece, albeit a flawed and very expensive one. Curiously for a film famous for its extravagances and alleged $44 million budget, the shoot in England was distinguished by running only £769.12 over budget, an amount attributed to the heroic intake of alcohol and cigars by three English film executives.

PART 2

THE COLLEGE BUILDINGS

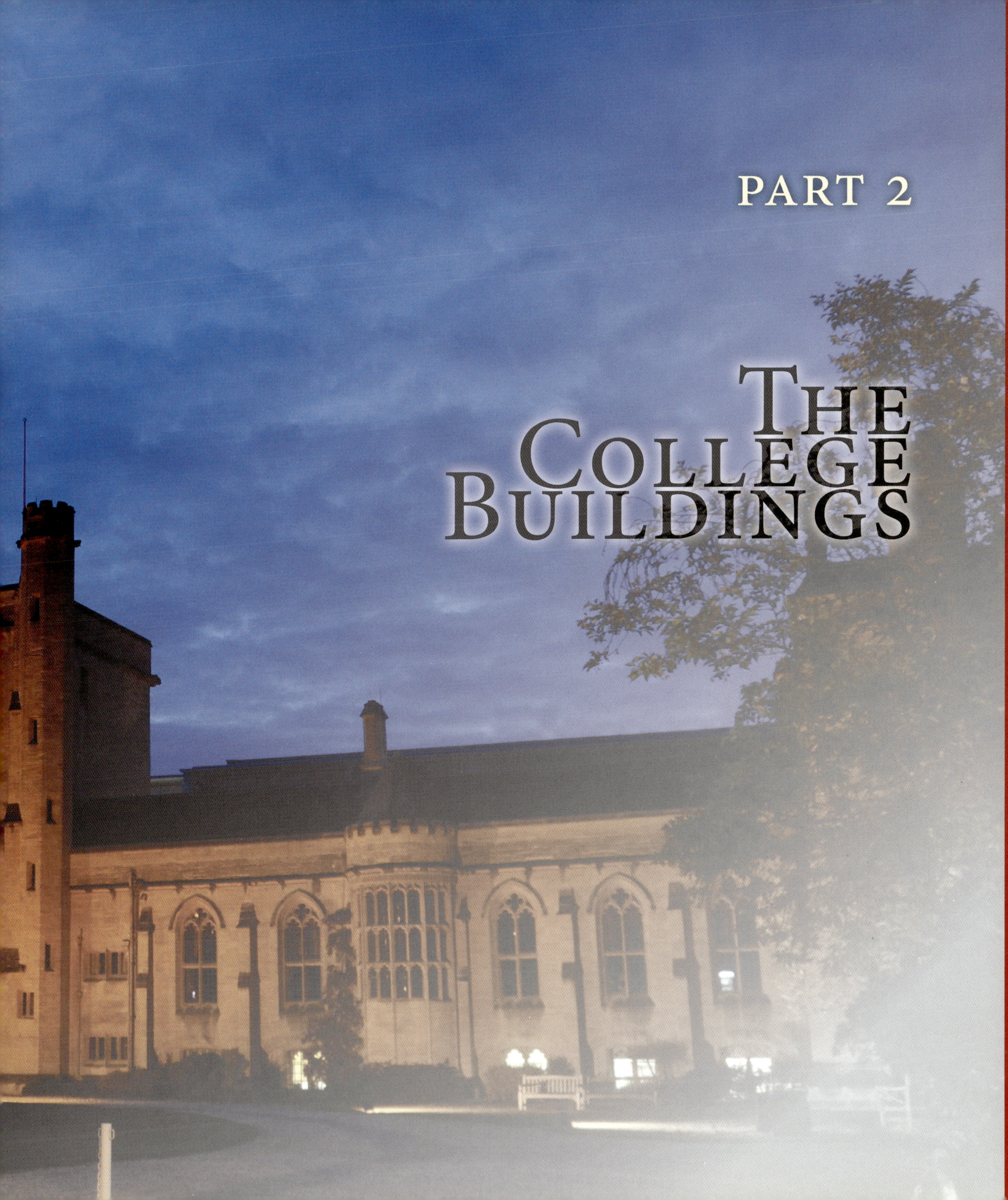

The Legacy of the Champneys Buildings

Michael Freeman

First-time visitors to Mansfield are often drawn to conclude that the College is a late-medieval one. Whether it is the decorated Gothic style of the chapel or the Perpendicular Gothic of the principal range, Mansfield has the look and feel of a 15th-century foundation. To its undergraduates and Fellows, of course, it is a lavish piece of late 19th-century Gothic Revival, although not at all what one might expect from a Nonconformist religious sect like the Congregationalists. But some have viewed the lavishness of its architectural form as a deliberate ploy by its founders, intended to beat the Anglicans at their own game or, at the very least, to show that they could compete on similar terms. The architect was Basil Champneys, and Mansfield is commonly regarded as the finest of his institutional designs. He secured the commission in open competition, Alfred Waterhouse providing the alternative scheme. On the wall of the Senior Common Room there hangs a watercolour of the Waterhouse entry. It had its main frontage on the road and, if built, would have appeared not unlike Harris Manchester College next door. It is clear that Champneys

Previous pages: The Champneys buildings.

Left: A view of the stately Perpendicular Gothic of Mansfield's main buildings.

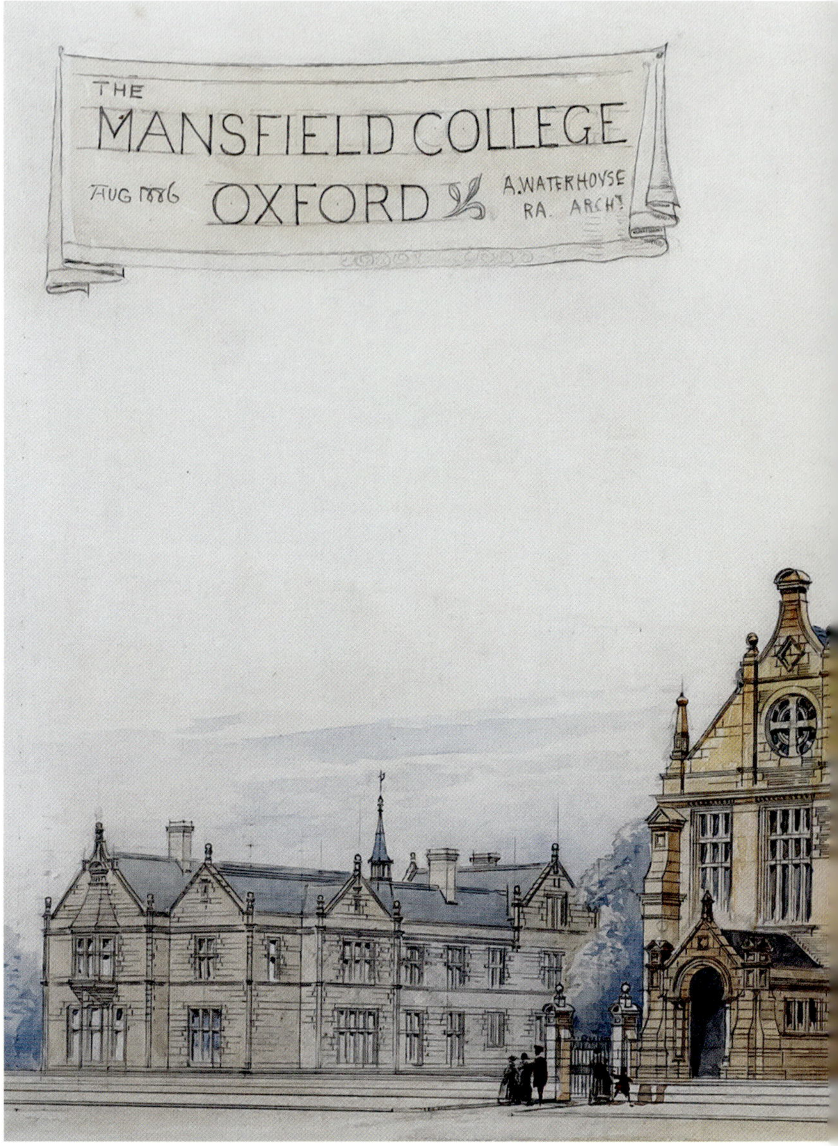

Alfred Waterhouse's alternative design for Mansfield, 1886. The watercolour now hangs in the SCR.

Basil Champneys (1842–1935) designed the new College in grand Gothic style.

offered by far the superior design, and so the College was erected over the years 1887–9 at a cost of £40,000.

As a piece of mock medievalism, the buildings have a powerful pedigree, for Champneys took his cue from the Hospital of St Cross, near Winchester, its principal buildings completed around 1445. Any Mansfield alumnus who ventures to visit St Cross today will not fail to experience a powerful feeling of déjà vu, for the gatehouse tower and adjacent ranges look uncannily like those of the College. The Hospital is famous for its 'wayfarer's dole' of bread and beer, so long-lost revellers from Mansfield's cellar bar will not go away unrewarded.

Mansfield was constructed of Oxfordshire limestone, Taynton stone to be precise, and although it is unfortunately not among the harder building stones, it has weathered to a fine shade of buff that

sets off the verticality of the building lines. However, Champneys' stroke of genius was to arrange the buildings at right angles to the projected new road. By producing an open-sided quadrangle (the open side to the south), anyone approaching from this point of the compass is presented with a remarkable vista: the grand Principal's Lodgings and library to the west, the soaring chapel to the east, and the gatehouse tower and hall in between. Prior to construction of the Thomas Rayson range in 1962 (the John Marsh Building), the view would have been yet more striking, for it would have emphasised the spacious land area on which the College was erected. As a Nonconformist foundation in Anglican-dominated Oxford, the open-sided quadrangle was powerfully symbolic, for as Fairbairn, the College's first Principal, observed, the founding intention was to attract through pulpit and professor's chair

Opposite: The SCR dining table in the hall.

Left: An early view of the baronial-style dining hall, with its oak-panelled walls and grand stone fireplace, designed by Basil Champneys.

Below: Detail of the fine wood carving in the library.

all branches of the evangelical churches in Oxford in a wholly unsectarian project. This feature has found broader echo in much more recent time with Mansfield's outreach programme, seeking entrants from schools and from social groupings that previously knew little of Oxford or Cambridge.

The downside of the particular orientation of Mansfield's buildings is that the gatehouse is not really a gatehouse at all, for it leads nowhere – other, that is, than affording access to the adjacent building ranges. There was once an outline of a scheme for it to lead into an inner quadrangle on the area now occupied by the chemistry building. However, the scheme foundered under Mansfield's consistent poverty.

Once inside the College buildings, there is yet more to savour. Pevsner regarded the library as a masterpiece of design, Champneys apparently taking inspiration from a medieval tithe barn at Harmondsworth in Middlesex. The internal timbering is most ingeniously done, according to Pevsner's description, creating naves, aisles and galleries under one huge roof. Around 1896 the library's ceiling panels were stencilled to an Arts and Crafts design, helping to create a strong sense of texture in what was otherwise a rather plain void. In the hall and Senior Common Room Champneys imitated a baronial style, complete with heavy oak panelling and grand stone fireplaces. Within the arch-braced ceiling panels, the Altrincham firm of George Faulkner Armitage (a distinguished Arts and Crafts enterprise in the mould of William Morris) added a whole sequence of Oxford college shields, the ones in the hall painted on plaster, those in the SCR on canvas. The same firm also designed much of the interior furnishing, some of which survives today, notably in the SCR.

Stone, stained glass and wood triumph in the chapel.

The hall at night.

The interior of the chapel is distinguished for its vast range of statuary and stained glass. Not only does this commemorate leading figures of the Reformed tradition across preceding centuries, but it also affords representations of many great figures of the Christian Churches more widely. Mansfield's chapel thus rejoiced in the inheritance of the whole Church and could confidently claim equality with other college chapels.

The unfortunate feature of Champneys' design for Mansfield was that it provided little in the way of residential accommodation for students. In fact, it was not conceived as a residential institution at all. When the College moved to the status of a permanent private hall (PPH) of the University in 1955, this became a serious problem, and efforts were immediately begun to raise funds for a new residential block. The south range by Oxford architect Thomas Rayson was the outcome, its northern elevation a somewhat bland exercise in Cotswold vernacular, the east elevation similar in form but also taking its cue from Edwin Lutyens, with its attractive staircase tower. It is faced largely in limestone and has careful architectural detailing, and Champneys would surely not have been disappointed with the addition to his grand quadrangle.

The Porters' Lodge

Duncan Forbes

'I pray you remember the porter'

Macbeth Act 2, Scene 3

Most Oxford colleges are entered through a tunnel. That is where the porters' lodge is typically to be found, both embodying and policing the boundary between inner and outer worlds. Within the college is the safe sanctuary of academia and arcane customs, preserved by the porter from the perilous contamination of Real Life (and, in the old days, of Women as well).

Mansfield begs to differ. Its claim to openness is, by historical accident, exemplified by the invitation from Mansfield Road of the spacious quadrangle. So inviting is it indeed that on at least one occasion tourists have had to be informed that the croquet mallets on the lawn are not provided for the use of the general public.

The College's desire to be both different from other colleges and at the same time fully part of the University – an aspiration which in times past bordered on ambivalence – is happily reflected in both the position and the style of its porters' lodge. Indeed, to the casual visitor, it might seem that there is no lodge at all. Where the porter now sits was originally the kitchen of a small flat, whose last resident is believed to have been Tony Lemon. From its window there is, perversely, no view of the main gate: before surveillance cameras were installed anyone wishing to pass in and

Mike Sherwood, head porter from 1987–2007, with Nigel Hall, a research fellow.

The porters' lodge was designed by Thomas Rayson as an integral part of the 1962 John Marsh Building.

out undetected could usually do so, as long as they remembered to keep close in to the lodge wall and to duck when passing the window. Mike Sherwood became adept at recognising Mansfield people (and not just students) by the tops of their heads.

It was different in Mansfield's first 75 years. Pevsner is a bit sniffy about the faux 'gatehouse' of the original building, but it does contain a porters' lodge in traditional style. At least, the word 'Porter' can be found on some plans of 1902, indicating the tiny room (with its bedroom above) that opens directly on to the entrance hall. For how long, if ever, this was used for its designed purpose isn't clear: the suspicion must be that the role of the college porter as currently understood became fully established at Mansfield only on the opening in 1962 of the John Marsh Building. The latter marked the first provision of student accommodation on the College site, necessary as a result of the College's achieving permanent private hall (PPH) status seven years previously.

As with the buildings, so with the staff. Taking their cue from the founding tradition, Mansfield porters have frequently shown a rich vein of Nonconformity. At no time was this more true than during the years of Mike Sherwood and of Hugh Flint, which spanned the 1990s with a generous overlap at each end. Two utterly contrasting characters, neither of them bore the slightest trace of the NCO, from which mould many traditional college porters have evidently, and not entirely happily, been poured.

Mike arrived at the College after a career with Imperial Chemical Industries. Looking for a way to pass his time after their PVC division was shot from under him, his first encounter with the College was when he called in for a discussion – rather than an interview – about the job, impressive with cravat and smartly rolled umbrella. His knowledge of railways was legendary and invaluable to anyone wanting to get to Holyhead or Hull. Of more use to the bursar was Mike's awareness of financial markets. Often after a review of the College's investments (such as they were) a

Barry Mawby, head porter 2007–12.

quiet word with Mike would confirm (or otherwise) that a sensible view had been taken. The College's reliance on US dollar income from students and conferences was, of course, obvious to Mike. In how many other lodges, I wonder, would the following exchange be likely to take place:

> Bursar: 'Morning, Mike. Dollar strengthening, I'm glad to say.'
> Mike: 'Good morning, Sir. Yes, it will be at £1.50 by the summer with any luck … On another topic, now would be a good time to sell Barclays, if the College has any shares.'

Music's loss and Mansfield's gain: Hugh Flint, former drummer for John Mayall and the Bluesbreakers, was deputy head porter from 1989–2005.

This would be followed by one of his familiar aphorisms. 'Life is full of small victories' – pause – 'and big defeats'.

If Mike represented the interests of Mammon, then Hugh as a Buddhist stood not perhaps for God but certainly for the transcendent. Hugh Flint, or Hughie as he was known in his musical heyday, was modest about his place in history, but he was a source of some awe to those for whom such names as Mayall and Clapton had resonance. When Hugh was on duty, dressed usually in fisherman's smock and sandals, discussion in the lodge would range widely. The results of his long conversations with students on topics of mutual interest were friendships that lasted for years.

In the second decade of the 21st century electronic devices now undertake many of the lodge functions for which a red felt-

Keep off the grass! – except when croquet is being played and the porter can relax.

tipped pen (one of Mike's most offensive weapons) used to suffice. But has the digital age usurped human contact? Barry Mawby, head porter at the time of writing, thinks not. He sees a continuity of values, sustainable through the small size of the College, whereby everyone connected with the place still feels themselves to be individually respected and valued. The term in *loco parentis* belongs to an earlier time, but for many contemporary students the lodge continues to represent a source of valued advice on matters ranging from when gowns should be worn to the stresses of being independent from home for perhaps the first time. Nor should it be forgotten that guidance may also be sought from the graduates whose employment as porters still upholds the polymathic tradition of the lodge.

Whatever their governing bodies might sometimes pretend, colleges have multiple centres of power, and the porters' lodge is certainly one of them. It reflects the ethos of Mansfield that its lodge is held in such respect and that its influence on the rest of the community remains wholly benign.

THE COLLEGE CHAPEL

John Muddiman

Mansfield College chapel – Oxford's 'cathedral of Nonconformity'. The word 'cathedral' may not be too strong a word to describe this amazing building. First, it is huge, one of the largest college chapels, intended as a place of worship not just for the 30-odd members of the College in 1889 but for each and every variety of Dissenter, newly admitted to the University, after centuries of exclusion. Second, it is a cathedral in another way: its central focus is the Principal's stall, more imposing than any episcopal throne. The Congregationalists rejected episcopacy, of course, but they put in its place the authority of a learned ministry. If one looks across the quad at the library, you pick out under its windows the letters SC-I-EN-TI-A; you have to go round the other side to find the complementary term TH-E-O-LO-GI-A.

Mansfield was built as a seat of theological learning and all the decoration in the chapel is intended to establish that claim. Its Nonconformist credentials are subtly hidden in this outstanding example of High Victorian Gothic.

The American stained glass window represents the close connection between Mansfield and the United States and includes the figures of William Penn, Jonathan Edwards, John Eliot, Roger Williams, Edward Winslow and Cotton Mather.

Stone-cut letters spelling out THEOLOGIA can be seen picked out beneath the library windows, mirrored by SCIENTIA on the other side.

As you enter by the main door, it is no surprise to find statues of the great minds of the Greek and Latin Church, Athanasius and Augustine, on either side; but look up and there is the figure of Origen, who inspired them both but who suffered the fate of posthumous excommunication for his disbelief in the eternity of hell fire. You don't have to be narrowly orthodox to be welcome here.

The statues inside, which are part of the original design, establish Mansfield's claim to be the champion of Protestant ecumenicalism. John Wesley greets you in the ante-chapel; but if you prefer your Methodism with more predestinarian bite to it, George Whitefield is third up on the left. There are other deliberate balancing acts among these impressive figures. Wycliffe, the 14th-century Oxford philosopher, is proleptically included as the 'morning star of the Reformation'; Luther faces Calvin at the far end, and John Knox,

The entrance to the chapel, with the dominating figure of Origen.

Revd George Whitefield (1714–70), one of the founding Methodists and an influential preacher of the Evangelical Revival in Britain and the Great Awakening in the American colonies. He was famous for his powerful pulpit performances and open-air preaching to mass audiences. His statue is in the chapel and the portrait (seen here) hangs in the SCR.

the fierce pioneer of the Scottish Reformation, guards the access to the pulpit on the right; as they make their ascent, preachers have to walk past him – his index finger, raised originally no doubt in a dire warning, has through time and happy accident dropped off, which may be taken as a parable for Mansfield's subsequent theological evolution. Among the lesser-known figures there are even early Anglicans, such as Richard Hooker, defender of the *via media* of the Elizabethan settlement, who refused to condemn the non-episcopal orders of continental Protestants. He is balanced by Thomas Cartwright, who would not have bishops of any kind. And there are other nice pairings: Richard Baxter, the gentle Puritan who stayed with the Established Church, and John Owen, who defended independency against both Episcopal and Presbyterian church government in Cromwell's day, and the latter's chaplain is included as less controversial than the Lord Protector himself. Music, which is such an important part of Protestant worship and for which this chapel was and still is renowned, is represented by Isaac Watts, the Father of English Hymnody. Thus, as long as you are not Catholic (Anglo or Roman) you have a welcome here, and an assiduous attempt has been made not to take sides in the internal disputes that so weakened the Protestant cause in earlier times.

The first Principal, Andrew Fairbairn, wanted the pulpit to be in the middle of the chapel, but it ended up to the side.

Past benefactors: Sarah Glover, widowed sister of George Mansfield, and Henry Manton, the Birmingham alderman who was instrumental in the foundation of Spring Hill College.

The stained glass windows in the chapel were added later. Facing north, rather than east, the far end depicts the prophets of the Old Testament and the apostles of the New, representing the primacy of scripture. The stylisations were standard for their time, but King David's bright red socks stand out as a nice touch. The authors of scripture witness to Christ, and up in the eaves – rather difficult to see and further obscured by the cobwebs – is the figure of Christ in glory. At the south end, in again rather standard Victorian style, are depictions of the call of the disciples and the feeding of the multitudes. This endorses the other key principle, the primacy of mission. Scripture and mission – the twin pillars of 19th-century Protestantism. Tucked away at the far end, you almost fail to see the little windows at the sides: to the left Sarah Glover, George Mansfield's wealthy widowed sister, who was persuaded by her brother to put up a sum of money for the original Spring Hill College before it moved to Oxford and took the Mansfield name; and alongside Alderman Henry Manton, the Birmingham silversmith, whose financial contribution is not known but must have been substantial to warrant a window of his own. This is a respectful nod to the College's past benefactors. But on the other side, two rather better known figures have an extraordinary little window to themselves: Plato alongside Amos. They represent, respectively, Greek rationality and the moral

The imposing chapel, decorated with statues and stained glass windows of key Biblical and religious figures, proclaims Mansfield as a serious seat of theological learning.

Hebrew social justice represented by the 8th-century BC prophet Amos and Greek rationality by Plato.

seriousness of the Hebrew prophets, the mainsprings of the European Enlightenment. The story that the other windows tell confirms this move towards a liberal post-Enlightenment form of pan-Protestantism, as we shall see.

The windows to the east and west are truly remarkable. The orientation of the chapel means that they catch the morning and the evening sun, and their colours have a gem-like brilliance. Although the Burne-Jones windows of the Virtues in Harris Manchester College are favoured by art cognoscenti, they pale by comparison to the windows in Mansfield. The first Principal, Andrew Fairbairn, was personally responsible for their choice and design, and he did quite a lot of research to try to find near contemporary likenesses. They were executed by the famous James Powell and Sons of Whitefriars, London, and installed in 1906, through the generosity

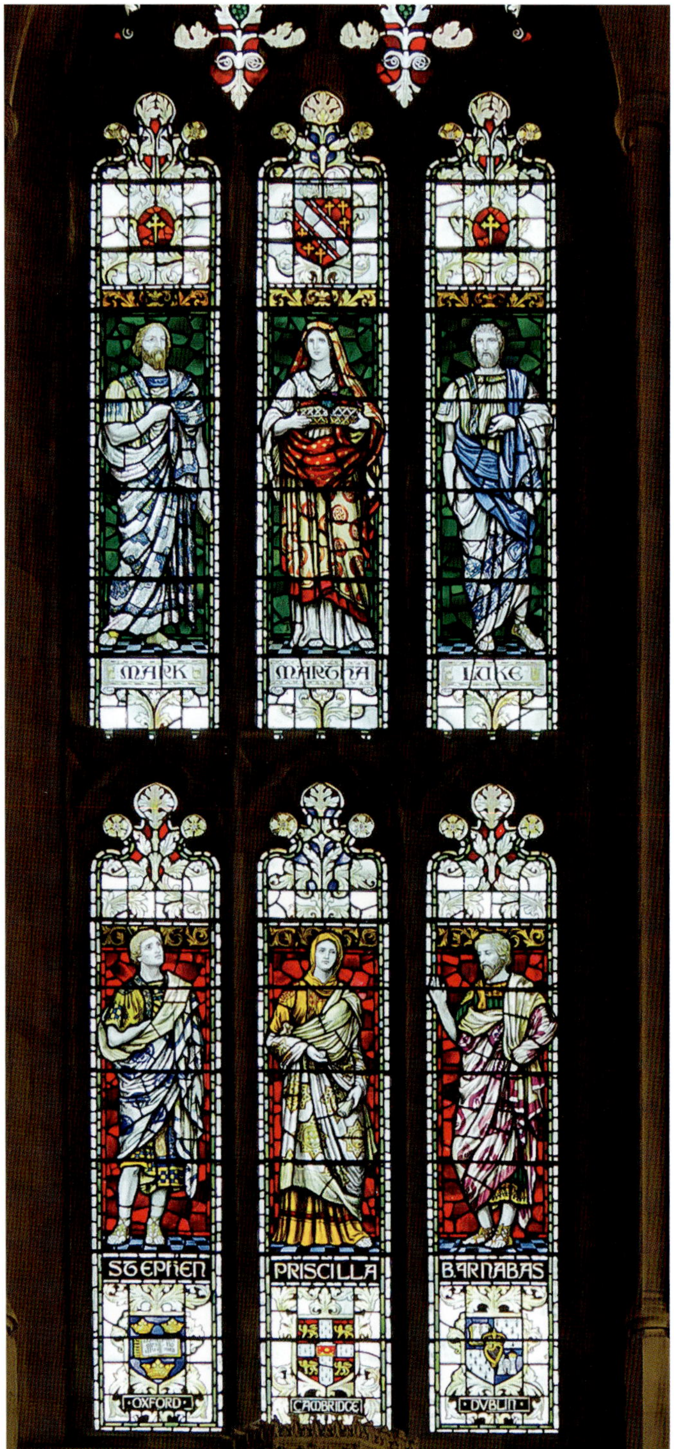

New Testament Evangelists Mark and Luke flank Martha, with beneath them Stephen, the first martyr, Priscilla, wife of the apostle Aquila, and Barnabas, Paul's fellow worker.

of Lord Winterstoke (formerly W.H. Wills of the Bristol Tobacco Company). (Smoking was perfectly acceptable in the early days of the College, while drinking was frowned upon by the majority of the students. It is the opposite nowadays.)

Taken together, before we look at individual portraits, they are a determined attempt to counter the accusation that Congregationalism was a recent innovation, an Oxford 'Johnny come lately' with no sense of the University's hallowed past. On the contrary, these windows claim for Mansfield the inheritance of the great 'catholic' tradition, which over time has become focused and purified to reach its present, self-confident, almost aggressive expression. As historian Clive Binfield writes, here 'the Catholic Church is looking in on the gathered Church'. Mansfield was basically intended to provide an alternative Faculty of Theology to the exclusively Anglican one hanging out in Christ Church, and these windows make a point: it is both more learned and equally more up to date than its rival.

The side windows are in roughly chronological order, with some linguistic/geographical groupings, going from right to left as one moves down the chapel from the far end. In the first are those New Testament characters not included in the north window: the two non-apostle Evangelists, Mark and Luke, are obvious choices; so is Barnabas, Paul's mission partner, and Stephen the first martyr. Less obvious choices are the women, Martha and Priscilla. There are no depictions of the Blessed Virgin Mary or Mary Magdalene anywhere in the chapel; two Oxford colleges were already dedicated to them (New College in the former case), so Martha is chosen instead, not probably for her domestic tantrum in Luke chapter 10 but for her considerable theological insight in John chapter 11. The

On the east side are Monica, mother of Augustine, with Tertullian, the first Latin Father, and Ambrose of Milan, his tutor. Beneath them are Jerome, author of the Latin Vulgate, Gregory the Great, and Patrick, apostle to the Irish, who sent a mission to England.

absence of any Marian iconography also makes an anti-Catholic statement (though there is now, on one side to make amends, a statue of the Virgin of Walsingham, which we know as Our Lady of the Radiator). Priscilla is here on her own; she seems to have been a more powerful figure than her husband Aquila described by St Paul as of note among the apostles, and it would not be long before the first woman minister in a mainstream trinitarian Christian denomination (Constance Todd) was ordained in Mansfield chapel in 1917. Admittedly, there are no post-Reformation women apart from the Quaker Elizabeth Fry; they were not well enough known.

As we go from side to side, the next window celebrates the heroes of the Greek Church, in addition to the two mentioned above who stand guard at the entrance. Irenaeus, Bishop of Lyon, attacked Gnostic heretics for their denial of the doctrine of creation; his polemic, as that of many early Fathers, is too ferocious for our taste, but he was trying to maintain a balance between creation and redemption, and he stands for a type of Christian thought that resists illiberal extremism. Clement of Alexandria wrote against pagan detractors and was probably the most cultured of the early Fathers. Eusebius wrote the first great church history; Chrysostom was a famous preacher; Basil composed the first monastic rule and a liturgy still used in the Orthodox Church. There isn't room for his brother Gregory of Nyssa, on whom our own Donald Sykes is such an expert. Helena, mother of Constantine, is the odd one out, not a theologian, but associated through her son with Christian imperialism and with various dubious legends about the discovery of the True Cross. She is matched on the other side by Monica, mother of Augustine, and further on we find Queen Margaret of Scotland, famous (apart from her piety) for giving birth to eight

View down the aisle to the carved oak stalls of the choir at the far end, and the imposing Principal's stall in the centre.

children. One cannot ignore the influence of monks and friars in the history of Christianity, but nuns would be too much – these were all respectably, if not always happily, married women. Perhaps that is why they were selected.

Back on the east side the Latin Church celebrates Tertullian, who laid down the terms in which the doctrine of the Trinity would be discussed in later theology; he was never canonised because of his heretically extreme asceticism, but you do not have to be an official saint to get into Mansfield chapel. Ambrose of Milan, the biblical commentator and hymn writer, is noted for his ability to read silently without moving the lips. Jerome, the author of the Latin Vulgate, is noted for being one of the most disagreeable people ever to have been declared a saint. There is Gregory the Great, the pope who sent Augustine to convert the English, and, balancing him, St Patrick, apostle to the Irish, who, along with St Andrew in Scotland, represents the other, non-Roman, Celtic mission to these islands, much prized in the Dissenting tradition.

When the present writer did Theology Schools in 1969 the Oxford syllabus stopped at the Council of Chalcedon in 451, so he is now moving into uncharted territory. The medieval church in Britain includes, of course, the Venerable Bede, whose church history was studied in the 1960s but only in history prelims. John the Scot, better known as Erigena, proposed the union of philosophy and religion and was suspected of pantheism for his pains. Duns Scotus famously defended the immaculate

Christmas carols led by the chapel choir.

conception (i.e. sinlessness) of Mary against Aquinas' objections. Bacon represents the union of religion with (the beginnings of) scientific enquiry in the medieval period. And Erasmus seems a bit out of place, since he was Dutch and a friend of many Reformers, but since he remained a Catholic he counts as medieval. His great contribution was to break the stranglehold of the Vulgate and return to the Greek text of the New Testament.

The window on the medieval church in Europe is a veritable splash of colour before the more sombre garb of the Reformers. The ecclesiastical vestments of these theologians are displayed in all their glorious detail. On the top Abelard and Anselm stand together, though they were miles apart on the doctrine of the atonement, and with them is Aquinas, the Angelic Doctor, whose works are studied in Oxford philosophy even today. Dante is there, one of Fairbairn's favourite authors, whose alabaster bust graces the library. And, of course, St Francis, who seems to be preaching to what looks like a budgerigar (though they were not imported into Europe until 1850).

The next two windows remind us of figures of the Reformation, some of whom it is easy to forget, but not Archbishop Thomas Cranmer, author of the original prayer books under Edward VI that are celebrated for their mastery of the English language; he was, of course, tried for heresy under Queen Mary and burned in the middle of Broad Street (Latimer and Ridley were equally martyred, but they were Cambridge men). The chief continental Reformers, Luther and Calvin, are already there in the statues, so here we have those of the second rank, like the Swiss radical Zwingli. Also included is Grotius, the jurist who propounded the theory of a just war.

Elaborate wood carving decorates a choir stall.

> *'They saw "Mansfield College", a new college just begun to be built, with such tremendously narrow windows that Isa was afraid the young gentlemen who come there will not be able to see to learn their lessons, and will go away from Oxford just as wise as they came.'*
>
> Lewis Carroll – 'Isa's visit to Oxford' (1888)

As you would expect, Cromwell appears in the Puritan window looking not too much of a Roundhead with his nice yellow tunic. We have a soft spot in Mansfield for the Commonwealth, though in most Oxford colleges Cromwell is remembered for blasting down the city walls after the siege of Oxford and appointing himself as Chancellor of the University. Milton, poet of Independency, also has a window, despite his prominence already in stone at the top of the tower; Mansfield is like a Paradise Regained.

Our American window deserves special note, for it had recent exposure to a wider public when it was used on fundraising literature for our neighbour, the Rothermere American Institute. But it was also a tribute originally to the close connection between Mansfield and the USA. Fairbairn was a frequent visitor and lecturer there. The presidents of Harvard and Yale sent congratulations at the opening of the College, welcoming the return of a Congregationalist institution like their own back to where it belonged. Of the six figures, one recognises William Penn (1644–1718), the Quaker who gave his name to Pennsylvania, but the others are relatively obscure, though Jonathan Edwards (1703–58), the president of Princeton, is enjoying a comeback in recent US scholarship. John Eliot (1604–90) was the missionary to the Massachusetts Indians; he translated the Bible into their language and published its first grammar. Edward Winslow (1595–1655) sailed on the Mayflower and was governor of Plymouth colony, and he was also reputedly a friend of the Native Americans. The Baptist tradition, so strong in America, is represented by Roger Williams (1603–83), another who wanted to keep on good terms with the Native Americans, though he had turbulent relations with his fellow Christians when he was pastor of Salem, where a generation later, in 1692, the infamous witch trials took place in which our last figure, Cotton Mather (1663–1728), became embroiled. Scholars are divided whether his interest in 'spectral evidences' fuelled the hysteria or whether he was a moderating influence. On the positive side, he was the champion of smallpox inoculation, against considerable opposition, in the Boston epidemic of 1721. None of these, with the possible exception of Edwards, could be called a great theologian, but they stand for the American memory, part myth, that if the Puritans had been left on their own the New World would have been a land of peace and freedom.

The chapel's lancet windows, which may have been those mistaken by Lewis Carroll for the narrow openings of poorly lit student rooms.

As you enter the ante-chapel, 18th- (on the right) and 19th-century (to the left) Nonconformists appear. It is difficult to see why some of them were selected, though there is a fair smattering of Scots, like Fairbairn himself. Thomas Chalmers (1780–1847), for instance, was the leader of the Free Church of Scotland and a prolific writer on political economy, defending capitalism and the law of supply and demand. There is a link between freedom of religion and the freedom of the market, albeit moderated by the moral duty of philanthropy. Even more surprising is the presence of Friedrich Schleiermacher (1768–1834), 'the father of modern theology', who contended that religion was based on intuition, more than revelation, and consisted in a feeling of absolute dependence. Fairbairn's colleague, W.B. Selbie, who succeeded him as the second Principal, was soon (1913) to publish an important study of this romantic liberal, which perhaps explains or is explained by its inclusion.

On the far side, apart from the genuflection to three prominent members of the College council, Dale and two more Scots, Hannay and MacKennal, there are two famous missionaries, also Scottish: David Livingstone (1813–73) to Central Africa and James Legge (1815–97) to China. Legge was a considerable scholar as well and became the first Professor of Chinese in the University, translating many works of Confucian and Taoist thinkers, and was open to other religious traditions, as was Fairbairn himself.

We have traced through this cavalcade a distinct evolution, from scripture to the Fathers, to the Schoolmen and the Reformers to the Puritans and the post-Restoration Nonconformists up to the present, when a moderately liberal but affirming Protestantism was heralded with the founding of Mansfield College as the only real alternative in contemporary Oxford to Anglo-Catholic obscurantism on the one hand and a despairing agnosticism on the other.

Deus Charitas est
Christus vos liberavit
Dominus fortitudo mea

The College Library

Alma Jenner

The College library is both beautiful and functional: 21st-century technology merges with the unique 19th-century Arts and Crafts design of Basil Champneys, who believed that architecture was an art, not a profession. An acquaintance of William Morris and Dante Gabriel Rossetti, he belonged to the Art Workers' Guild and divided his time equally between art and literature. The elaborate wood carvings, by master carver Robert Bridgeman of Lichfield, and the attractive stencilled panels by Powell's of Whitefriars, which together decorate the great pitched roof, were created under his direction. His attention to detail can be seen in the quirky carved owl or the green man peering through gilded foliage from a ceiling boss, the birds and mythical creatures in the reading bays, or the pretty oriel windows and linenfold carving on the library cupboards.

The library design, resembling a medieval barn with great oak posts holding up the roof and the gallery, is thought to have been inspired by the tithe barn at Harmondsworth, Middlesex, although Nikolaus Pevsner took a more ecclesiastical view

The great pitched roof of the library, ornamented with stencilled scrolls and Latin mottos, is studded with carved bosses.

verba Dei
Qui ex Deo est

Top: Portraits of clergymen ejected from the Church of England by the Act of Uniformity in 1662 hang above the study bays.

Above: An early photograph, c. 1890, in the library gallery, before the ceiling panels were stencilled.

Opposite: Champneys' magnificent library.

and described the library as having a nave with the study bays as aisles.

Champneys' masterpiece was soon inhabited when Spring Hill College, Birmingham, closed and the book collections were moved to Oxford to become the foundation of Mansfield library. Five hundred volumes still survive and include books from the library of Congregational preacher, John Angell James, some interesting letters on the abolition of slavery (bearing penny black and penny red stamps), as well as the Spring Hill archive.

Many important bequests were received in the 1890s, when J. Vernon Bartlett was librarian, including Migne's *Patrologia* and valuable theological and philosophical collections from the libraries of R.W. Dale, Henry Rogers and Daniel Proctor. An endowment from William Hinmers JP of Manchester enabled many new books to be purchased. Anglican friends in Oxford were also generous, with donations from the library of Dr Edwin Hatch, Reader in ecclesiastical history, and valuable palaeographical works from Canon Sanday of Christ Church. Presentations of a different order were the books on temperance, which included such titles as *The Illustrious Abstainer* and, from Mr Joseph Rowntree, *The Temperance Problem*. However, the distinctive characteristic of the original collections is identified in the works of the early Nonconformists that document the history of their struggles and subsequent ejection from the Anglican Church. Portraits of some of these great and principled men hang from the gallery in the main library and in other parts of the College.

During the following decades a succession of eminent Fellow librarians, including G.W. Thatcher, Alexander Souter,

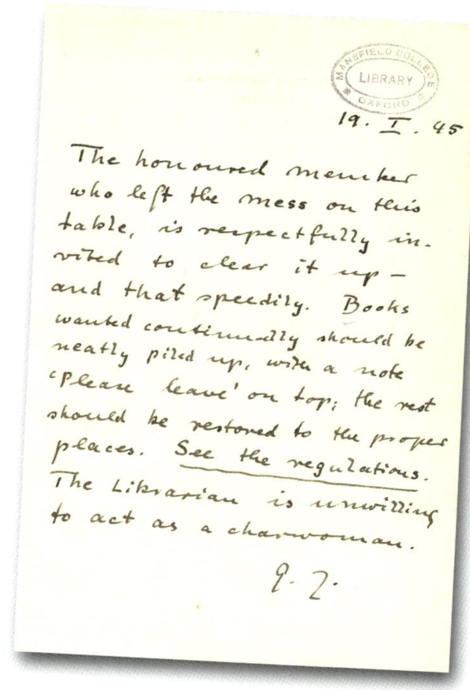

19. I. 45

The honoured member who left the mess on this table, is respectfully invited to clear it up – and that speedily. Books wanted continually should be neatly piled up, with a note 'Please leave' on top; the rest should be restored to the proper places. See the regulations.
The Librarian is unwilling to act as a charwoman.

G. Z.

Librarian Gunther Zuntz courteously laying down the law in 1945.

James Vernon Bartlet, Professor of Early Church History, was also librarian in the 1890s. (From Mansfield College Caricatures 1906 *by W.H. Coats.)*

W.A. Davies, C.H. Dodd, C.J. Cadoux and Erik Routley, attempted to deal with the constant stream of library donations as well as the new accessions. Many volumes remained stacked high in corridors or languished on the library landings. The JCR was called upon repeatedly to move books, clean shelves, catalogue and re-catalogue according to successive 'ingenious' numbering systems (one of which has been adapted and remains in use today). Various attempts were made to house and sort the books. The small classroom nearest the library was shelved by Heal & Son of London in 1906 to house J.B. Paton's library of church history and Principal Fairbairn's theological and philosophical bequest. (The snooker table held court here for a number of years surrounded by dusty journals and pints of beer.) The 'Prophet's Chamber', a room for visiting pastors and now the library office, was also used as a stack room. Perhaps the greatest attempt to create order was made during the war years, when all the books were taken to New College library after the government requisitioned the College. Librarian Dr Gunther Zuntz, 'one of the ablest and most delightful refugee professors', tried to sort out the chronic overcrowding and catalogue the extensive Vernon Bartlet bequest. Ten thousand books were extracted, and after the war a 'shadow library' was assembled in the old air-raid shelter on the north wall of the main corridor for books not much used, and the residue went into the two classrooms on the library landing. All this stock was eventually sold or offered to other libraries, including the Bodleian, in the 1960s and 1970s, under the librarianships of Basil Yeaxlee and retired Congregational minister Gordon Trowell, who also organised the disposal of extensive journal holdings.

The Law Library, lined with oak bookshelves, houses the law reports and working collection of history books.

Until the late 1970s Mansfield was predominantly a male theological college with some students reading English, history, law and geography; there was an occasional woman ordinand and fewer than a hundred students. The library office was a temporary structure on the upper library landing, which had been built by the JCR in 1955 from work cubicles left over from the war. The only comfort was an electric bar fire, and catalogue cards were produced on a portable Hermes typewriter. The main library had war black-out blinds covering the upper windows, fluorescent strip lighting boxes hung on chains attached to wooden constructions suspended across the book bays, and there was seating for 16 readers. Students sometimes signed flimsy slips to register the loan of books.

In 1983 the Council Room, on the lower library landing, was re-located to the ground floor so that a reading room could be provided for the expanding student numbers. At first there were four tables and a free-standing bookcase; it took 20 years and a generous donation of OUP money for it to reach its full potential,

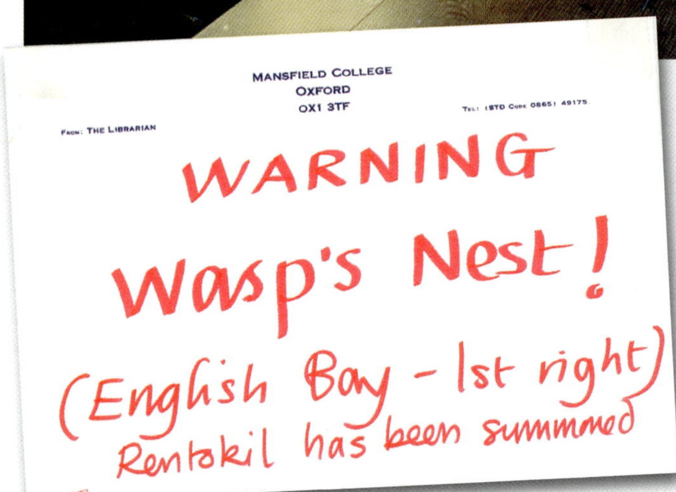

Mansfield College
Oxford
OX1 3TF

Tel: (STD Code 0865) 49175.

From: The Librarian

WARNING
Wasp's Nest!
(English Bay - 1st right)
Rentokil has been summoned

The unanticipated hazards of scholarship.

which includes specially designed oak tables fitted with internet connections and low-level lighting, comfortable chairs, computers and electronic catalogues.

In 1997 Mansfield became one of the first College libraries to catalogue the library holdings electronically and to introduce an automatic borrowing system for readers, moves that signalled further years of improvement and expansion. In 2001 the Middle Common Room on the library landing re-located to the tower, and a law library was established. This small, handsome room has been entirely lined with high oak bookshelves, which hold the law reports and a fine working collection of history books; it has become another favoured study area.

Press cuttings are carefully preserved.

'Mansfield's library is unique: there is none in my experience that matches the aura and air of learning in such a peaceful yet stirring environment. The Victorian ceiling and Puritan portraits help create the atmosphere, as does the quality of light, when so many more libraries think windows an irrelevance. Alma, the Librarian, also contributed to our studies by being a never-failing source of ideas and inspiration.'

D.W. (BILL) THOMAS – *1985, THEOLOGY*

Alumni have been generous in funding the purchase of a number of the bespoke chairs in the libraries which replicate Champneys' original design.

Mansfield now has a stock of over 30,000 books, a suite of three libraries and a book-purchasing policy that aims to provide the core texts in all subjects the College offers for undergraduate study. Readers have 24-hour access to a comfortable working environment, and in addition there is an adjacent computer room with printing facilities.

In spite of all the dispersals and the lack of storage facilities, the library has managed to retain the core of its inheritance of material for the study of English and Welsh Nonconformity, a valuable number of antiquarian books and a range of original donations, including a first edition of Locke's *Essay Concerning Human Understanding*. Other treasures include a 15th-century manuscript of an Italian missal and a collection of early printed

One of the College treasures: the manuscript of a 15th-century Italian missal.

24 Chalfont Road,
Oxford.
3 June 1907.

Dear Rix,
I have felt it my duty to inform the Principal that I encountered you on your way to the river yesterday morning, at a time when you ought to have been attending the last Sunday communion service of your college course.

Yours sincerely,
A. Souter.

The spiritual confronts the worldly. Note from Professor Souter to E. Wilton Rix (pictured), a theology student at Mansfield from 1904–7.

Bibles. Conservation work on the antiquarian volumes has been undertaken by Frederick Cooper, the library binder for many years. The folio volumes are in a reasonable condition, but numerous leather bindings need further attention when funds permit. The antiquarian stock has been listed and independently valued, but more work is needed to catalogue it professionally and make it available to research scholars.

In 2009 the latest dispersal of books took place when the ordination course ceased after 123 years. A 'Mansfield Collection' was created from the volumes retained.

The Mansfield Archive, the main repository for official College records, is housed in the library. It was founded initially on a few early minute books, College reports and photo albums. Material has been collected (some may say extracted) from all departments over the past 30 years and includes architectural and historical information; College minutes, reports and magazines; JCR minute books and smoking concert programmes; chapel and library archives; biographical folders and oral histories of members; and the Mansfield House settlement reports. Unique items continue to be donated by alumni or their relations, including First World War letters sent from Gallipoli by E. Wilton Rix, a book of caricatures of College Fellows dating from 1906 by the son of Alan W. Stevens (Mansfield student in 1903), boat club memorabilia from Wally Buckingham, and John Marsh's Hebrew typewriter.

An extensive photographic archive was established separately in 2005 and is housed on the library landing in two handsome wooden plan chests. A representative amount of material has already been digitised.

Mansfield now has a fully fledged Oxford college library. The transformation from an exclusively theological library has been gradual, with its roots being retained in the old collections, and documented in the archives. The stewardship of its architecturally lovely rooms is continually challenging, but we must trust that future generations of Mansfield's students honour and care for the library that President Jimmy Carter described as 'truly the most beautiful'.

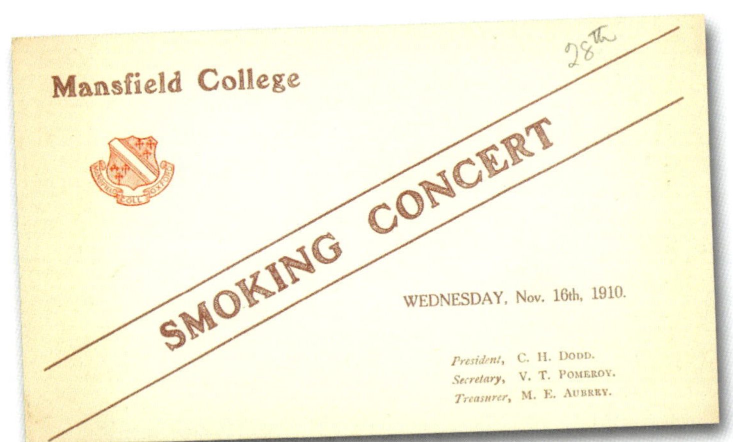

The Mansfield Archive is the repository for College records of all kinds.

Among those featured in the album of Mansfield College Caricatures 1906, *drawn by Mansfield student W.H. Coats (1903–7), were the Principal, Andrew Fairbairn, James Vernon Bartlet, Professor of Early Church History and librarian, and George Buchanan Gray, Tutor in Hebrew.*

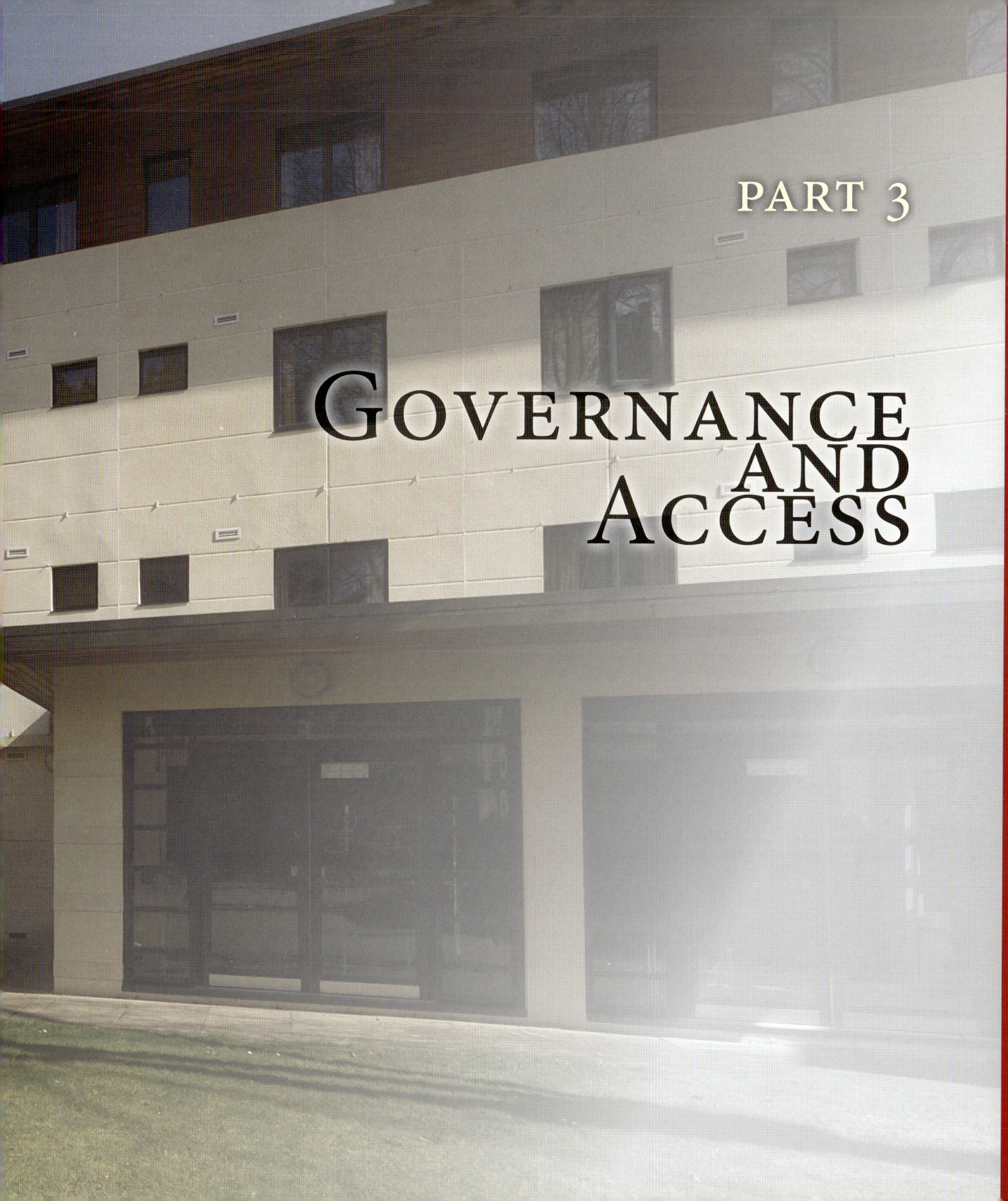

PART 3

Governance and Access

1932

May 13.

COLLEGE DOCTOR

BREAKFASTS IN HALL.

GEORGE STREET

Dr SELBIE

The question of the s
was considered, and it was
appointment.

The Principal spoke
the students, that breakf
day. He felt that this
College greatly. His h
might follow breakfast, s
9 o'clock instead of 10,
work might begin earlier,
said there were difficult
tion and staff, but he w
as to the possibility an
culties at the next Coun
anxious to meet the Prin

A letter was read f
Church, Oxford, declinin
lecture room for a part

A letter was read f
tional Union thanking th
for the Spring meetings
England and Wales.

It was unanimously
the title of Principal E

The Bursar reported

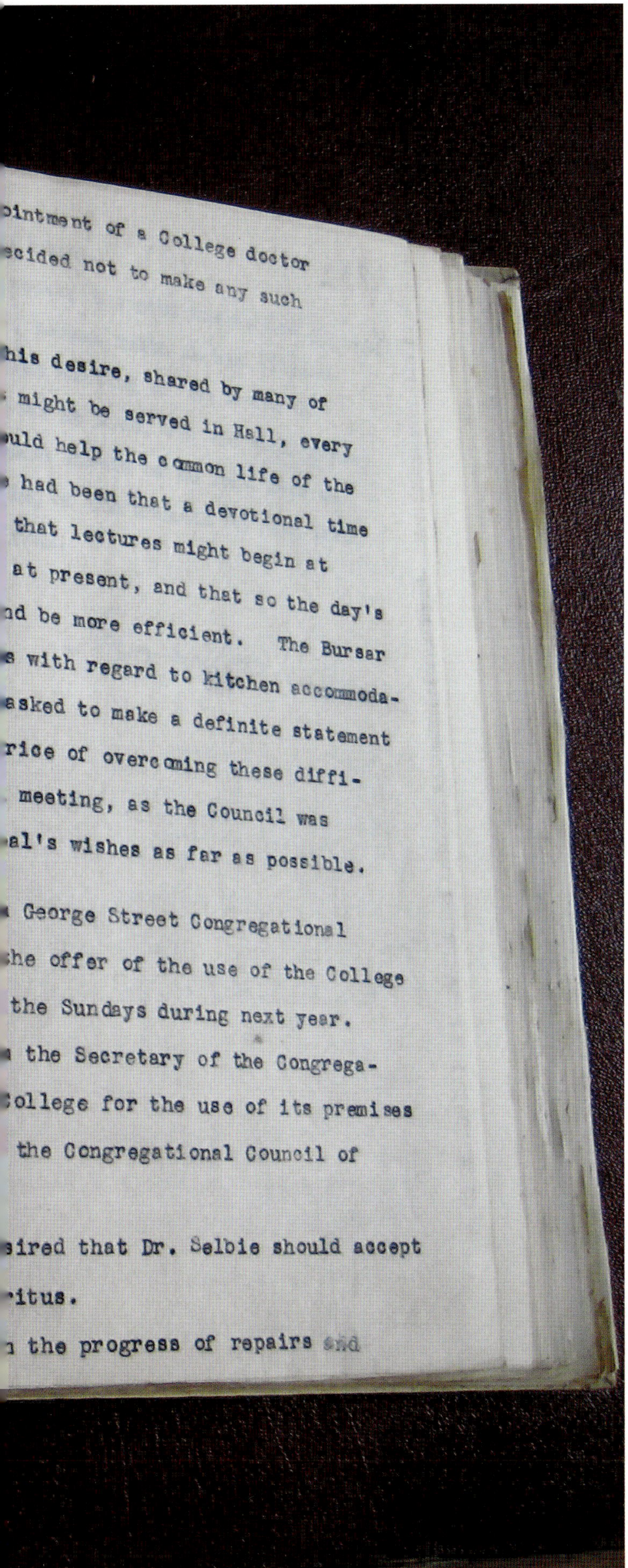

Governance and Administration: Glimpses of Mansfield's Journey

Tony Lemon

Coming to Mansfield in 1969, I soon realised that the College was very much in transition. Non-theological students had been admitted since Mansfield became part of the University as a permanent private hall (PPH) in 1955, but they had been taught largely by tutors based in other colleges. At one point, apparently, no fewer than 17 honour schools were represented, but English was the only non-theological subject to have Mansfield-based tutors (from 1960, and a Fellow, John Creaser, from 1966). This was to change following publication of the Franks Report in 1967. This self-commissioned enquiry into the University was critical of colleges taking undergraduates for subjects in which they did not have their own Fellows, making Mansfield feel particularly vulnerable. From this stemmed the decision to focus on a few subjects and elect Fellows in them, which led to appointments in history, law and geography in the next few years. Theologians – ordinands and undergraduates – were a minority of the intake from 1963 onwards, but the constitution remained that of 1886, and the governance of the College hovered

Previous pages: The Garden Building.

Left: Minutes of the College Council record the wide range of issues discussed, as demonstrated in this extract from May 1932.

Freshers and tutors, October 1979.

awkwardly between constitutional requirements and day-to-day realities. In the SCR academic tutors were outnumbered by up to 12 academic visitors, many of them American theologians, but these played no part in College governance.

The governing body was the College Council, meeting three times a year. Financial matters were controlled by a largely external finance committee, and ordination training was formally the responsibility of the Board of Education. SCR meetings were (blessedly) short and discussion limited. In my first year I recall John Marsh, who had courageously sought to move Mansfield in the direction of a normal undergraduate college, reporting on his conversations with the then four Anglican theological colleges with a view to all four moving to the Mansfield site – how different the College might have been! In this transitional period there was considerable uncertainty about many things: for example, the new law Fellow, Anthony Ogus, arrived to find that the implications of the term 'Fellow', which appeared in his job advertisement, appeared not to have been formally considered. As a lawyer, not surprisingly, he moved quickly to have the subject discussed and the position regularised. Matters in the bursary were also remarkably ad hoc, and budgets were frequently incomplete at the beginning of a new financial year. 'New subjects' were sometimes the object of curious perceptions: the librarian's report of February 1977 says of the classification of politics and economics: 'These

The College trustees, shown here after their last meeting in 1995, played an important role in College governance before full college status was granted.

I have regarded as "background" subjects – the modern state to balance the ancient world around the Mediterranean.'

Mansfield's relationship with the University and the colleges was fragile and uncertain. When John Marsh approached the Vice-Chancellor in 1966 about the College seeking a charter he met a discouraging response, as this was viewed as implying that Mansfield was seeking full college status. In order to make the College better known, new Heads of House and new professors in subjects relevant to Mansfield were entertained in groups at occasional special guest nights from the late 1960s onwards. Our first attempt to join the colleges admissions system received a firm 'no' in 1973. Attempts to expand undergraduate numbers often flowed against the tide of government and University policy (though the former fluctuated wildly), and Mansfield was subject to a PPH statute permitting no more than ten undergraduates to live outside college accommodation. Joint appointments with the University were not possible for PPHs, and the University made no contribution to Fellows' salaries, despite happily accepting their contribution to lecturing and examining (not to mention the fees of the undergraduates they taught): George Caird's New Testament lectures had long been the mainstay of undergraduate teaching in theology, and the new Fellows quickly made their contributions. John Marsh's decision, approved by the College Council, to press ahead with the election of non-theological Fellows was thus made in faith – just about affordable when they were young, but soon to present problems as they moved up the salary scale. A joint approach from the five PPHs to the University was made in 1972 concerning eligibility for CUF lecturerships (joint appointments in which the University paid nearly half the salary), but it was not until 1982, following another approach, that a favourable but limited response was received in the form of three 'special (non-CUF) lecturerships', two of which came to Mansfield's English and geography Fellows. Only in 1995, with full college status, was justice done in the form of joint appointments for all Mansfield's existing academic Fellows.

The SCR

As the SCR grew in size and the Fellows in experience, the de facto centre of gravity in College governance moved steadily from Council to SCR. Donald Sykes sought to spread responsibilities among the Fellows, making John Creaser Vice-Principal and Senior Tutor, Tony Lemon Tutor for Admissions and Mike Mahony, Dean. Other roles, such as Tutor for Graduates, Tutor for Women and Fellow librarian, came later as Mansfield became increasingly like other colleges. Two Fellows plus the Principal and bursar attended the finance committee, and all Fellows could attend Council meetings – only two of them as voting members but this mattered little as the Council invariably decided by consensus, as did other bodies.

Tony Lemon combined his role as Tutor in Geography with other administrative positions in Mansfield, which included shouldering the burden of managing the wine cellar.

Occasionally such diffused decision-making could prove problematic, as in 1982 when a deposed bursar took Mansfield to an industrial tribunal (unsuccessfully) on the grounds that notice of termination should have been given by the College Council. Minutes of Council meetings also reveal a degree of randomness in the things reported – undergraduate academic results, for instance, appear only three times in the years 1971–88. New appointments are usually noted, but appointing procedures and names of those involved are often absent. Names and items often crop up with little explanation. Such omissions reflect an increasingly marginal relationship between the Council and the day-to-day reality of College governance.

Despite differing emphases and preoccupations, mutual trust and goodwill generally prevailed, and the system worked, even if some Fellows heard similar reports and discussions three times over. With the now amusing exception of the finance committee's initial refusal to allow the purchase of a photocopier, SCR views were respected, perhaps most notably on two occasions of potential conflict: the first in 1976 when, following representations in a Council meeting, Fellows were allowed to constitute the majority of the search committee for a Principal to succeed George Caird; and the second in 1984, when Council minutes refer diplomatically to 'frank and wide-ranging discussions' on the roles of the finance committee and the bursar. The major de facto involvement of the

Mike Mahony, Tutor in History and Acting Principal 1988–9, about to advise his students.

Fellows in critical aspects of College governance is clearly evident – for example, Richard Buckley played a critical role regarding the new constitution, Tony Lemon chaired the appeal steering committee in the early 1980s, and Mike Mahony served as Acting Principal in 1988–9.

Two themes consistently dominate Council minutes: financial problems and constitutional change. The former were not assisted by the rapid succession of bursars in 1981–6, but thereafter Duncan Forbes brought much-needed stability, good humour and the optimism that is essential for all Mansfield bursars. In Council meetings the need for endowment was repeatedly stressed but little achieved until the 1980s. Several exercises in financial stringency – sadly still very much a part of College life – are recorded, including decisions to charge for the Commemoration dinner and move the bursary to the College entrance so as to dispense with porters (1975) and to end Sunday meals (1976). The experimental appointment of a part-time bursar in 1981 proved short lived. Negotiations with the JCR about board and lodging charges were often difficult, though only once, in 1987, did the generally good relations between Common Rooms fail to prevent a rent strike. A centenary appeal from 1981 onwards, directed by Peter Spicer, an old friend of the College, allowed necessary renovation of the Champneys buildings and made some contribution to endowment, but operating deficits occurred in most years during the 1970s and 1980s.

The financial gloom of the early 1980s was briefly relieved by the £41,000 (equal to two years' deficits) received from United Artists for *Heaven's Gate*, on which Tom Lancaster writes elsewhere in this volume (see pages 52–3). In a rare specific reference to financial matters, Council minutes of October 1984 note the increasing volume of Mansfield's conference trade and the increasing proportion of profit in the gross turnover.

A New Constitution

The 1886 constitution was obsolete in many respects, including the absence of any mention of non-theological teaching, which by 1973 was three-quarters of the College's work. George Caird stressed to Council that a new constitution was essential if new endowment was to be raised, emphasising that: 'Any new constitution must be such as would not prevent Mansfield eventually becoming a full college of the university.' Matters ground slowly, and it was only in 1983 that an exploratory meeting with the Charity Commission took place. Two more years passed before a detailed response was received to Mansfield's proposals, but by May 1986 Council felt able to make the necessary formal request for the Charity Commission to make a trust scheme, at the same time formally recording its desire 'to move as quickly as possible to receiving a Royal Charter and to seeking full college status within the University of Oxford'. The two things were separate, however: the new constitution became operative in late

The College crest.

1987, replacing Council with a body of trustees and constituting the Fellows as the Governing Body. With characteristic confusion, Council minutes move from reference to the 'SCR' in 1986 to 'Governing Body' in May 1987, with no explanation of this change of terminology some months before the new constitution became operative.

Alongside these financial and constitutional struggles, the academic character of Mansfield progressed rapidly, as is recorded elsewhere in this volume. In 1988, following a massive effort in which letters were sent to each Governing Body member in every college, Mansfield became a full member of the colleges admissions system, which led to steady growth in first-choice applicants. This and other things, notably the achievements of the Fellows, enabled Mansfield to pass the (unspecified) academic criteria for college status well before it surmounted the financial hurdle. Indeed, the latter was not so much surmounted as by-passed when government policy had moved towards expansion of student numbers, and acceptance of Mansfield as a full college in 1995 occurred more quickly, in the end, than generally expected.

What difference has college status made? Psychologically, it meant an enormous sense of achieving a fundamental goal, an end of the need for endless explanations of PPH status and the confidence to go forward as a full member of the club. Financially, it brought long-overdue University contributions to Fellows' salaries but no immediate help from the College Contributions Fund (CCF), whereby rich colleges help the poor. This was delayed until 2001, when a new scheme was introduced, and Mansfield successfully argued for its inclusion. The benefits were considerable, enabling rapid growth of endowment (albeit to a level still far behind most colleges), but since 2008 have been limited to grants for recurrent expenditure, with the recent introduction of yet another scheme under which the wealthy colleges and the University have paid once-for-all capital sums into the fund. Academically, it meant improved undergraduate and, increasingly, graduate applications and somewhat reduced institutional constraints on the growth of the student body. It has also allowed Mansfield to compete on equal terms with other colleges for joint appointments, including University chairs, which has led to the continuing growth of the fellowship and with it a welcome expansion of the size and expertise of the Governing Body.

Governmentally, college status placed full responsibility on the Fellows, as in other colleges – this time de jure as well as de facto. An outside observer would still note differences between our procedures and those of older colleges: a less developed committee structure and associated tendency to discuss matters at length in full Governing Body; an academic policy committee that, although a sub-committee of Governing Body, has a larger membership than Governing Body itself; the continuing absence of the by-laws envisaged in 1995 and associated procedural uncertainty at times; and the tendency to reach decisions by consensus rather than formal voting, something that may need to

change in an enlarged Governing Body in order to give all Fellows a feeling of fuller involvement.

In sum, college status represents the end of a long struggle but the beginning of a new era, with both continuing challenges and new opportunities. Mansfield's narrative is the fascinating story of a small but complex and rapidly changing college and its relationship to an ancient university. With slender finances but rich human resources, the College has reached the point where it can, while retaining its traditional values and respecting its theological heritage, hold its head high among Oxford's colleges. Our founding fathers would, I think, have rejoiced to see the journey Mansfield has made in its first 125 years.

'It is only with the benefit of hindsight that I truly realise just how fortunate I was to have been given the gift of attending Mansfield College. Opening my acceptance letter from the college over twenty years ago (standing with my parents in the checkout line in Tesco, don't ask...), was one of the best days in my life. As the first person in my family to go to university, it was a "big deal". My tutors Tony, Pam and Michael were unrivalled: they challenged, they criticized, they expected a lot ... and I am the beneficiary of their selfless investment. I have wonderful memories of my time at Oxford and many life-long friendships – including my wife Catherine, who I met at the Oxford Union in my first week.'

Giles Harrison – *1986, Geography*

EVER CLOSER UNION
The Material World
The Force of Poetry

Access to the College: The Further Education Initiative

Lucinda Rumsey *and* Janet Dyson

There is a neat synergy between Mansfield's current reputation as a college dedicated to widening participation to Oxford and its beginnings. Its original foundation as a college for students who had previously been excluded from an Oxford education, and its buildings standing open to the world with no high enclosing wall, suggest that it is appropriate that we are known as the 'access' college. In its recent history Mansfield has had to put more effort than most Oxford colleges into recruitment and undergraduate admissions. When we were a permanent private hall (PPH) we were relegated to the back of the University prospectus, and when we gained full college status we were still small and little known; not many candidates listed us as their first-choice college. Our tutors had to become practised at finding promising candidates who had applied to other colleges but had been overlooked by tutors picking from a much larger pool. We also played an active part in the scheme run by a number of Oxford colleges in the 1980s, offering places in PPE to applicants from Inner London Educational Authority

Encountering a wider world.

The Access to Excellence Campaign was launched by David Marquand, the Principal, in 2000.

schools that had little experience of sending students to Oxford. Our experience of unearthing overlooked talent put us in a strong position when we came to set up an outreach project of our own.

The Access to Excellence Campaign launched by the then Principal David Marquand in 2000 was built on what we felt was a cornerstone of our mission as a college: making an Oxford education available to all those clever and hard-working enough to benefit from it, regardless of educational background. The Further Education Access Initiative was a central pillar of this campaign. A working group set up in 1999 and led by Ros Ballaster, Tutor for Admissions, concluded that students from the further education (FE) sector were under-represented at Oxford. In 1999 Oxford received only 379 applications from general further education colleges, and the success rate for these students was significantly lower than for those from other education sectors. As well as the low application and success rate from general further education colleges, it was noticed that tertiary colleges and sixth form colleges also sent fewer applicants to Oxford than other groups in the state sector, and it was recognised that all further education students face particular challenges: the large size of these colleges, sometimes on different campuses, makes it difficult for staff to disseminate information, and class sizes are also large; institutions offer a variety of qualifications beside A levels and the International Baccalaureate; additionally, many cater for mature students who have different challenges in applying to university.

Perhaps most importantly, all students in the sector have experienced a fracture in their education at the age of 16 and have known their tutors for only a year before they make their university applications. It was felt that an outreach project aimed at this sector could have a significant impact on applications to Oxford. The research undertaken by Janet Dyson, who as the new Tutor for Admissions in 1999 was responsible for establishing the project, ensured that it responded sympathetically to the needs of the sector. One key factor in this was a conference held at Mansfield in September 2000 for FE college principals to launch the project officially. This provided information about applications to Oxford, with question-and-answer sessions and demonstration interviews, but also started a dialogue with the FE sector about how application and success rates for candidates from the FE sector could be improved.

However, if the access initiative was to be successful, there would be far more new applications than a college of Mansfield's size could accommodate, and thus, rather than going it alone, Harris Manchester, Hertford, Keble, New College, St Hugh's and Worcester were invited to join Mansfield in convening a further education consortium, which pledged to work closely with FE students and staff in order to help candidates make better informed university choices, and also to encourage them to apply to Oxford. Mansfield itself set a goal of raising its own intake of students from the state sector (at that time it was 58 per cent, which was already much higher than the University average) to 75 per cent, including five students each year from the FE sector. In its first year Mansfield awarded places to ten students from the sector, indicating that the potential scope of the initiative was even wider than first thought.

Michael Freeden with a student.

The proposal clearly also struck a chord outside Oxford, and Peter Lampl of the Sutton Trust and a representative from Atlantic Philanthropies actually approached Mansfield to talk about offering support. Generous alumni gave the £60,000 matching funds that were required. This enabled a full-time recruitment officer, Janine Fisher, an Oxford graduate, to be appointed to manage the project. After Janine's departure in 2003, Helen Etty, also an Oxford graduate and a former further education college student, took over the post of recruitment officer alongside the new Tutor for Admissions, Lucinda Rumsey. Careful husbanding of the funds and additional subscriptions (offered by the consortium colleges from the third year onwards) enabled the project to expand its work.

Last-minute preparation for a tutorial.

From modest beginnings the Further Education Access Initiative grew to become the University's largest outreach project. It maintained annual contact with staff and students in over 400 FE, tertiary and sixth form colleges across the country. Up to 200 annual events were held in FE colleges in England and Wales, providing information about life at Oxford and the application and interview process. At a time when widening participation work across Oxford University was burgeoning and more colleges were hiring their own access officers, the work done by Helen Etty and her assistants, first Lynn Featherstone and then Danielle Cluer, made up nearly half of all the outreach activities undertaken by the University as a whole. In 2005 the Chancellor, Chris Patten, acknowledged its importance to Oxford:

> One of the most important and imaginative initiatives that Oxford has taken in recent years to widen participation is the work that Helen Etty of Mansfield College has been doing to encourage students from further education and sixth form colleges to apply for entry to the University. Thanks to this work applications have been increasing and the success rate has gone up. This is the result of a great

Right: A student study-bedroom.

Below: Mansfield student Miguel Hilario-Manenima – the first member of the Shipibo-Conibo people ever to leave the Amazon jungle to study – won a Rotary International scholarship to Oxford to read politics and economics in 1998.

deal of hard work involving visits, conferences, speeches, open days and e-mentoring. I very much hope that this vital work will continue to flourish.

The cycle of activities each year began with higher education fairs and outbound introductory talks for interested year 12 students and their parents, as well as visits to Oxford for groups of students. Regional information days for potential applicants were run jointly with Cambridge University, using one FE college as a host and inviting all other colleges from the area. Personal statement and application workshops followed, and for students who made an Oxford application, an extensive programme of interview workshops during the autumn term of year 13 and larger-scale interview information days in Oxford, which were designed to reassure students about the nature of Oxford interviews and inform them about the process.

A key focus of the project was encouraging students to see the value of non-vocational degrees. The humanities study days enabled 300 sixth-formers each March to spend a day in Oxford and study in a small group with a tutor as an introduction to the tutorial system.

An annual e-mentoring scheme matched over 100 FE students from 75 colleges with current Oxford students who shared their subject interest and could give informal advice and information about the University. A mentee from John Leggott College in Scunthorpe who was successful in gaining a place at Oxford wrote: 'I had an e-Mentor when I applied, and it really helped. Thanks for all the help from the access initiative; I really do think it made an incredible difference. I would credit it as the difference between me getting a place and not.'

The FE open day, which was first held in 2003 for 150 students, has grown to an annual attendance of 250 students and, owing to the increased demand, a further event, the sixth form college open day, has taken place each year since 2005. The success of the first teachers' conference for FE staff in 2000 led to a biennial event

Students relaxing in the quad.

for up to 100 participants, giving the opportunity for FE staff to engage in discussion with Oxford tutors. The initiative developed a dual purpose: working with high-performing colleges to provide targeted events to encourage students to apply to Oxford, with the aims of raising Oxford's intake from the state sector and of engaging with and supporting colleges with little experience of Oxford applications to ensure that all prospective FE applicants and interested staff could access up-to-date and accurate information.

When Oxford, along with many other universities, asked to charge undergraduates fees of up to £3,000, it was required to sign an Office of Fair Access agreement, committing to widening participation to previously excluded groups and describing the ways it was achieving this. Oxford's OFFA agreement cited the FE initiative as 'the most significant of Oxford's access programmes' and Aim Higher, HEFCE's national programme for widening access to higher education, named it 'one of the key influences on young people's higher education decisions in the northwest of England'.

In 2008 the FE initiative broadened the scope of its work from FE colleges themselves to their feeder schools in order better to advise year 10 and 11 students about choosing A level subjects that would help them make competitive applications to top universities.

The initiative was unique in being a college-run and college-funded project. It was originally planned and funded to run for four years. The Oxford colleges in the consortium contributed £2,500 a year to the running costs, and staff and student volunteers from every college contributed to events. After the initial years, the original seven colleges in the consortium were joined by Jesus, Pembroke, St Catherine's, St Edmund Hall, St Peter's, St John's and University College.

The consortium quickly grew to 27 Oxford colleges and continued to run for two more years, entirely funded by their contributions. By 2009 applications to Oxford from FE colleges had increased by 77 per cent since the initiative's conception, and applications from sixth form colleges had grown by 48 per cent over the same period. The number of offers made to students in the FE and sixth form college sector had also increased as a proportion of overall offers to the maintained sector.

In 2009 a new structure of access work across the University began, as each Oxford college was given particular regions of the UK in which to concentrate their access work. Mansfield had to consider whether to continue with its work exclusively with the FE sector or whether to pick a region and begin a new project. It seemed a good time to start something new. We asked to be allocated a region that we knew had one of the lowest application and success rates to Oxford, the East Riding of Yorkshire, and we were also allocated an area of Kent, including Bromley and Croydon. We proposed that the FE sector should be included in regionalisation and all the Oxford colleges take responsibility for the FE colleges in their area. Mansfield retains two of the initiative's largest events, the FE and sixth form college open days, and runs

Adjusting a carnation on the way to Finals.

these events in Oxford annually. Helen Etty moved to become Mansfield's academic administrator and oversees Mansfield's access work with an admissions and access administrator. We still do a lot of work with FE and sixth form colleges, having made many friends over the years, but it has been interesting to make a new start to our access activities. In the past we did not go out to FE colleges recruiting applicants for Mansfield; we were doing this project for the consortium and the University. It makes a nice change to concentrate our efforts for the first time on recruiting candidates for Mansfield.

We have come a long way since the FE initiative was launched. It was with some pride that we recently responded to a Freedom of Information request about the access work we had undertaken between 2005 and 2011, sending back a list of over 1,700 events. Many of the access events we introduced over the years have become the standard for access events run by many Oxford colleges, and we continue to think of innovative ways to make Oxford and Mansfield open to the world. In 2011, 85 per cent of our first years were from the state sector, by far the highest figure achieved by any Oxford college.

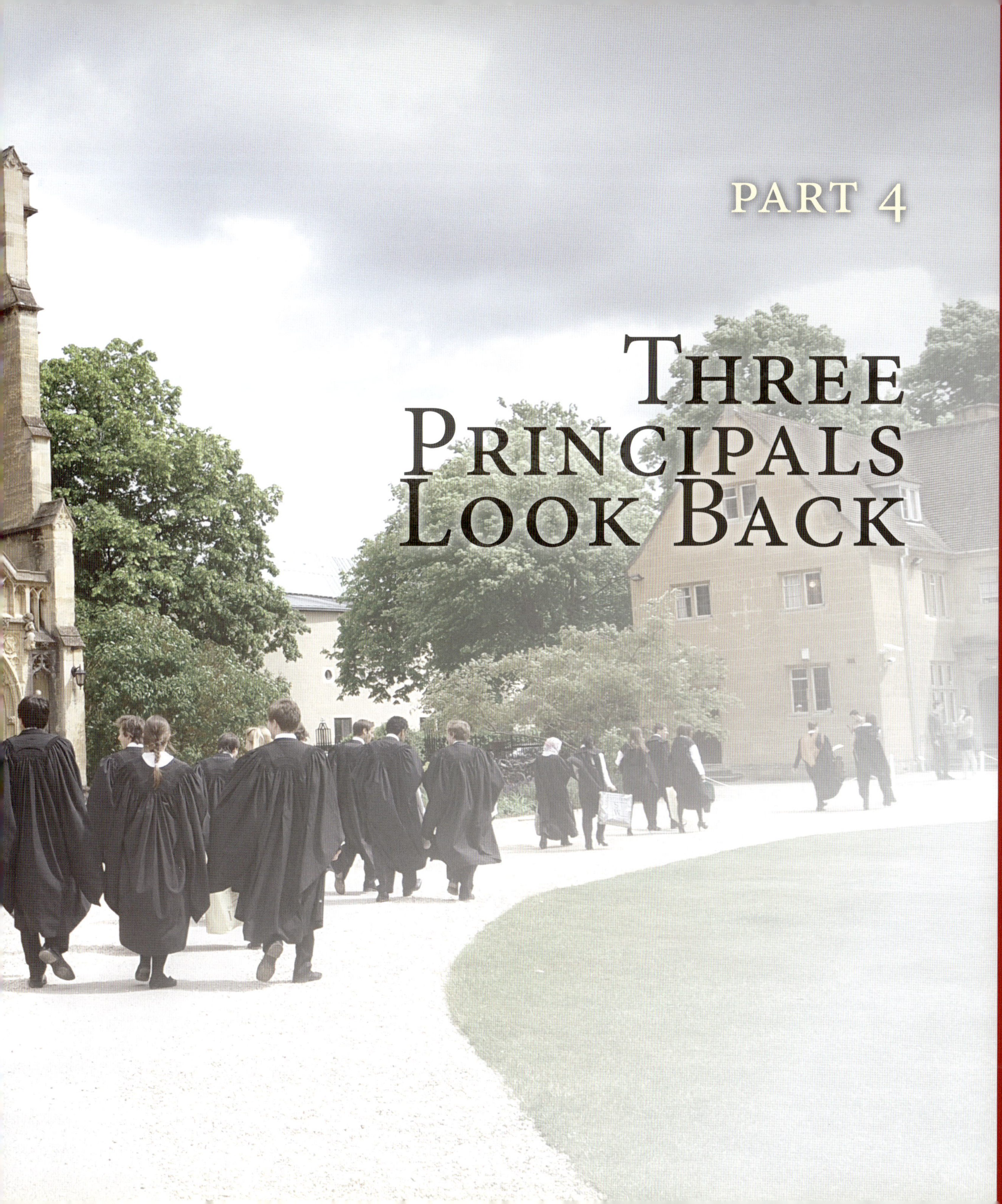

PART 4

Three Principals Look Back

Theology

Donald Sykes

When I decided that I wanted to read theology, one of the attractions of Mansfield was the context in which theology was being taught. The subject was not being studied in seminary fashion, in isolation, though I recognised the existence of first-class seminaries. At St Andrews I had become accustomed to reading my subject, classics, alongside students in many subjects. In halls of residence I did meet other classicists, but always alongside medical, engineering, English and history students and many more. This was my first encounter with students in theology, taught by distinguished teachers at St Mary's College, but sharing social and cultural life with the rest of us. Student life there was also quite international. My neighbour for several years came from Ghana, and every continent was represented.

Mansfield had been in origin a college for graduates who then read theology as a further subject, either through the respected Mansfield course or by taking the University degree. By the time I came up in 1955, however, the College had been for two years

Previous pages: En route to the Sheldonian.

Left: The Theology Library, seen here in the mid-1980s.

Donald Sykes, the sixth Principal of Mansfield (1977–86).

a permanent private hall (PPH) of the University, educating students in an expanding range of subjects. The range was still comparatively small, but it was significant for me to study theology not only with students who would go on to ordination or to teach religious education but also with those reading, say, English, history and law. John Marsh's vision was keen to add sciences, and students in these subjects, though few, added to the intellectual breadth of Mansfield.

Breadth, however, needed to be considered in another respect. For generations the honour school of theology had been noted for its depth rather than the breadth of its scope. It called for concentration and precision, with an emphasis on language, but allowed little opportunity (except in optional additional subjects) beyond developments up to the year 451. (I recall being teased about having taken a degree in 'Christian Archaeology'.) This changed when new regulations not only allowed, but called for, the study of Christian thought into the 20th century, allowing also for a coverage of philosophy and religion and a comprehensive range of other religions. At the same time the degree retained its

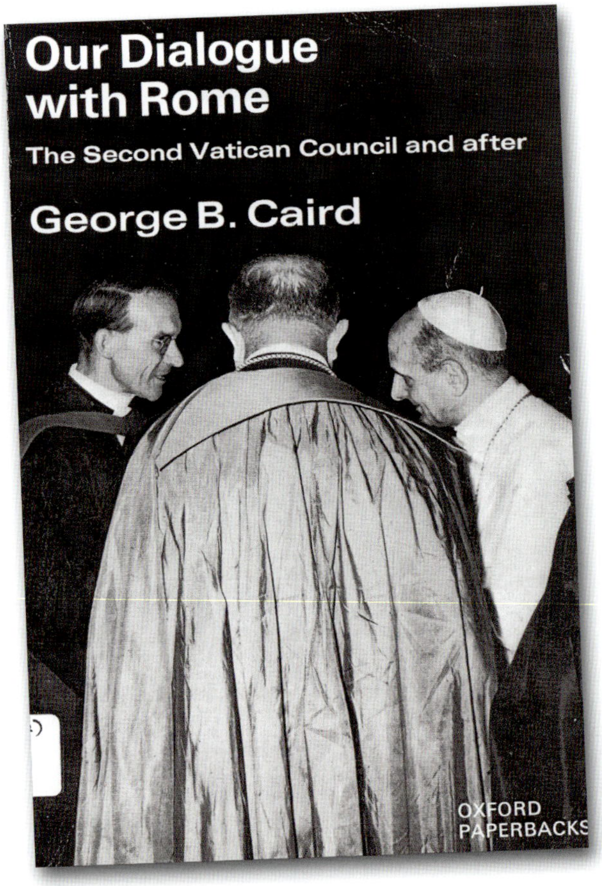

George Caird, fifth Principal of Mansfield, represented the Reformed Churches as official observer at the Second Vatican Council (1962–5). The cover photograph shows him being presented to Pope Paul VI.

Ordinands Susan Pierce and Michael Durber in the MCR, c.1980.

traditional strengths. The coming of the joint degree in philosophy and theology was an initiative that attracted a number of able students. Another innovation was the introduction of the Certificate in Theology, offering a viable option to the honour school, to be followed by the degree of Bachelor in Theology, now taken by a number of our students and widely regarded as a firm foundation for continuing study. Mansfield had always been strong in candidates for advanced degrees in research, the B.Litt. or M.Litt., BD and the degrees of B.Phil., M.Phil. and D.Phil., alongside distinguished scholars who obtained the DD.

One result of these changes was a widening of the range of students studying theology. It became clear to many that the subject was one that offered an education in its own right to those who did not intend to pursue it in a professional way. As a teacher, I found this a stimulating development and privilege. I am grateful for what I have been able to learn from generations of students in this and other colleges whom I have been allowed to teach.

Andrew Fairbairn with Fellows at a theology conference in Marburg. (From Mansfield College Caricatures 1906 *by W.H. Coats.)*

ELIZABETH THE SECOND
by the Grace of God of the United Kingdom of Great Britain and Northern Ireland and of Our other Realms and Territories Queen, Head of the Commonwealth, Defender of the Faith:
TO ALL TO WHOM THESE PRESENTS SHALL COME, GREETING!

FULL COLLEGE STATUS

Dennis Trevelyan

When I was, to my great delight and complete surprise, elected Principal of Mansfield College I was left in no doubt that my overriding priority should be to seek to obtain full college status for Mansfield. This had been a College ambition for some years, and Lord Bancroft, an outstanding chairman of the trustees, who played a quiet but vital role throughout the subsequent negotiations, stressed its importance. I said, unwisely but accurately, that I should have failed if, during my period as Principal, I did not achieve this objective. The quest was on.

Mansfield College became a permanent private hall (PPH) in 1955, a status devised for theological colleges. These colleges met together every month, and I felt much at home as they discussed current political issues in accurate, if somewhat irreligious, terms. But Mansfield College had outgrown its theological origins following the wise decision of John Marsh, its then Principal, to enlarge its teaching base to disciplines outside theology. As a PPH, Mansfield College was on the periphery of University

Dennis Trevelyan and Lord Bancroft displaying the College Charter, 1995.

The College motto: Deus locutus est nobis in filio *('God hath spoken unto us by his Son').*

activities, playing little or no part in determining the policy of the University. It also suffered financially since, given its status, it was deprived of access to the College Contributions Fund (CCF), a financial mechanism by which the richer colleges subsidised the poorer ones.

The University was not unsympathetic to Mansfield College, but if it achieved full college status other PPHs might follow the lead with, as the University saw it, incalculable financial implications. Admittedly, the University had laid down conditions that, if satisfied, would lead to the College's admission. These were that we should, among other things, not only have a vision for our future but acquire a fund of £5.5 million (at July 1988 prices) and put up two-thirds of our students in College-provided accommodation. To demand impossible conditions was, I suppose, a polite method of refusal.

What was clear was that if Mansfield College was to achieve its objective, it had on the one hand to take a much more significant part in University activities and on the other to alter the nature of the argument for and against its admission. On the first point, a good deal had already been done. Apart from the active and successful part that the College's students had taken in University social and sporting activities, remarkable work by Donald Sykes and Michael Mahony made it possible to persuade the University to allow the College to have its own spokesman (the other PPHs had only one spokesman for them all). The College was already engaged in major building projects, and the complicated process of setting up the Oxford Centre for the Environment, Ethics and Society. As Principal and possibly because of my civil service background, I was invited to become the chairman of a review of the organisation of criminological and social legal studies, and I also became chairman of the University Equal Opportunities Committee. At the same time, my wife joined the committee of the Newcomers' Club, an organisation that looked after the interests of families of foreign postgraduates. The University was also provided with a list of the achievements of our teaching staff. (It was a list of impressive academic distinction.) It was plain that Mansfield College could hold its own with other colleges and, even more important, could not be ignored.

The Principal, Dennis Trevelyan, with Archbishop Desmond Tutu in 1995.

At the same time, however, we had to alter the nature of the argument about our admission. The conditions laid down for admission could not be achieved. Instead, we deliberately sought to face the University with the need to explain why Mansfield College was not a full college and in what ways it was different from other small colleges in the University. The University reacted by setting up a study of our finances that soon showed that we had conducted ourselves with financial prudence. Our work on our building plans amply demonstrated that we had a real and realistic vision for our future.

The University was obliged to look again at our case. Above all, we could count on the sympathy of Sir Richard Southwood, the then Vice-Chancellor, without whose support we should have had little hope of success. There followed a lengthy and Byzantine series of discussions leading to procedures in Congregation, the Charity Commission and finally in the Privy Council. The objective was to enable a joint petition of the College and the University to be made to the Privy Council, which was necessary before we could become a full college. It was, however, first necessary to revise our own statutes so that they were appropriate for a full college and, even more difficult, to incorporate amendments lately required. Richard Buckley and I laboured on the necessary amendments – it was like a Ximenes crossword but more complicated – but finally a corrected draft became available. (It is interesting that another college that gained full college status adopted our draft.)

The Queen gave her consent to the petition on 31 May 1995, and the College 'Charter Day' was a rainy 24 June 1995. It was attended by the Chancellor, Lord Jenkins. Thereafter, benefits

'I loved the fact that Mansfield wasn't just for ordinands, but that we were among "ordinary" students, from the beginning working out our beliefs in discussion with geographers and linguists, poets and physicists. We were constantly aware that we were to do our theology (and our socialising) in a real-life setting: a placement in Littlemore Hospital taught me much about getting one's hands dirty in the service of others, although it was with the more able patients mending bikes in my case – the old radiogram in the ward had only one record, the Wombles' LP, and hearing those songs again brings me straight back to the smell of the grease.'

D.W. (BILL) THOMAS – *1985, THEOLOGY*

came our way. For example, the number of students we could admit was increased by the University from 132 to 162, and distinguished members of the College were given University appointments, to the financial benefit of the College. But, above all, Mansfield College moved from the periphery of University affairs to the centre. For example, I was elected to be the chairman of a committee of smaller colleges, which was in a position to play a significant role in University affairs, and my successors have played an important part in such matters.

But these are battles long ago. It is, however, significant that we were the first undergraduate college to become a full college for 30 years and, even more important for us, Mansfield was the first college with a Nonconformist background to have been made a full college of the University. It has been said that Nonconformity has come of age. Full college status has proved beyond doubt that there was no way in which Mansfield College could be distinguished from other small colleges in the University. But I am glad to say that there is widespread agreement that we should nevertheless retain our reputation 'as a small, friendly and informal college, solicitous about the welfare of students and enthusiastic about academic and sporting life'. We previously lived for all intents and purposes on the edge of the University; we are now inside it. In the undergraduate prospectus we lodge between Magdalen and Merton (to the greater glory of them both).

Opposite: Aerial view of Mansfield College, c. 1980.

Behind the Green Baize Door

David Marquand

Two early memories first. Just before taking up the reins of office (if that is what they were) I asked Anthony Smith, President of Magdalen and a sometime student contemporary, if he had any advice for a rookie head of house. 'Always remember two things,' he said. 'There is no honeymoon period. And behind that green baize door is another green baize door.' Tony's first warning was wrong. I had fallen in love with Mansfield and its tradition of sturdy, occasionally slightly zany Nonconformity, when I was summoned for inspection by the Governing Body, months before my job interview. (How could I not be in love with the only Oxford College to have a portrait of Cromwell hanging in the place of honour in its SCR?) The love affair lasted. Being Principal of Mansfield was a permanent honeymoon, the most enjoyable and worthwhile job I've ever had. But Tony's second warning was well founded. When I ventured into the wider University, the place positively bristled with green baize doors. Kafka had nothing on Wellington Square.

The Principal's study.

The SCR provides the Fellows with the opportunity for an occasional restful interlude.

The portrait of Oliver Cromwell in the SCR, a gift from William Crosfield in 1889, is a Florentine copy of Sir Peter Lely's painting of 1653, which hangs in the Pitti Palace, Florence.

My second early memory is also about doors. After a long day getting our furniture into the Victorian splendour of the Principal's Lodgings, Judith and I were tired and hungry. The then steward, Robin McGarry, served us a heart-warming dinner, with a nice bottle of wine, in the SCR. By the end we were tipsily happy. Imagine our horror when we discovered that, before leaving the College for the night, Robin had locked the door to the SCR and left no key. We could get from the SCR into the hall, but the door from the hall to the outside corridor was also locked. It was out of term, and no students or Fellows could be seen. By dint of frenzied gestures and agonised shouts to passing conference attendees we eventually got a message through to the porters' lodge and were duly rescued. But it was a close run thing. The University's green baize doors were as nothing compared to Mansfield's sturdy Victorian oak.

Highs and lows. The lowest low came a year into my principalship, when the newly installed Blair government

abolished the famous (or infamous) college fee. As a citizen, I couldn't object. As head of the poorest college in Oxford, I was petrified. It seemed to me entirely possible that the College would go bankrupt and that I would be the last and most inglorious Principal of a distinguished line. I now realise that I was more worried than I need have been. In its disorganised, but splendidly human way, Oxford does look after its waifs and strays. But I didn't know that then, and in any case the role of waif did not appeal.

The highest high came when Guy Hands, our one seriously rich alumnus and our most munificent donor, handed me a cheque for £2 million, made out to the College, in the middle of a taxi ride in central London. I was terrified I'd lose it, and told him so. 'Don't worry,' he said. 'No one else can cash it.' So I went back to Oxford with it burning a metaphorical hole in the inside pocket of my jacket. I wasn't really at ease until it was safely in the hands of the almost equally nervous bursar, Duncan Forbes.

In 2001, David Blunkett (centre) delivered the first Hands Lecture entitled 'Learning, Citizenship, and Equality in the Twenty-First Century'. He is seen here with (from left to right) David Marquand (Principal), Guy Hands, Colin Lucas (Vice-Chancellor), and Julia Hands.

As all this implies, money was an abiding preoccupation. I wasn't just a fundraiser. I also spent long hours fighting Mansfield's financial corner in a host of University groups. There was, I remember, a Monday Group, a Thursday Group and even a Friday Group, all concerned in one way or another with more-or-less filthy lucre. There was also a Recipient Colleges Group, consisting of poor colleges in receipt of help from rich ones by way of a mysterious institution known as the College Contributions Fund (CCF). By a bizarre twist of logic worthy of the medieval Schoolmen who helped to found the University, Mansfield was too poor to qualify for CCF disbursements at the start of my term of office, but it was allowed into the group and treated very graciously by the other members. And in the end, we made it into the CCF system, a few months before my retirement. Decades of importunate nagging, latterly by me and earlier by a long line of my predecessors, had finally paid off.

Money wasn't everything, however. Sadly, I didn't have time to do any undergraduate teaching, but I did supervise a couple of graduate students, and Judith and I threw frequent parties for students, graduate and undergraduate, in the Lodgings – a

superb venue for any kind of jollification. If that sounds frivolous, it shouldn't. Colleges are the heart and soul of Oxford, and colleges depend on collegiality, buttressed by jollification, as well as by more solemn activities. The hours that my magnificent PA, Jane Buswell, and I devoted to bringing interesting visitors in to College guest nights were well spent. I look back with particular pleasure to visits by Michael Frayn, the one undoubted genius among my oldest friends, and by Jeremy Paxman, who turned out to be warm and wise as well as witty.

At least one solemn activity was even more enjoyable. Because Mansfield did not become a full college of the University till 1995, only a year before I became Principal, my term of office saw a steady expansion in the size of the fellowship. One of the greatest delights of my role was a close involvement in a number of new appointments. I knew nothing whatever about some of the subjects concerned, and I had no expertise in any of them, but listening to the ebb and flow of probing and forensic interviews, in which up-and-coming young scholars batted ideas back and forth with world-class authorities in their disciplines, was a fascinating experience, intellectually and psychologically. No names, no pack drill. But I don't think I am betraying any confidences in saying that I was awed by the mathematicians, dazzled by the lawyers, humbled by the physicists, captivated by the economists and thrilled by the theologians. Most of all, I was proud of Mansfield – proud both of the calibre of the candidates we were attracting and of the zest that the eventual appointees brought to the intellectual life of the College. Mansfield was on the march, I used to reflect at the end of these interviews. And I still think I was right.

We were on the march in another sphere as well. Thanks partly to Guy Hands' generosity, partly to his social conscience, partly to the lateral thinking of the then development director Nick Blinco, partly to the advice and support of the Vice-Chancellor Colin Lucas, and most of all to the enthusiasm and commitment of the College fellowship, we were able to launch a ground-breaking project to widen access to Oxford from the FE sector. We recruited a consortium of colleges to support us – some centuries old, like New College, others newer, like Harris Manchester – and won funding from the Sutton Trust to appoint an access officer, whose task was to preach the gospel in FE colleges up and down the country. Mansfield was founded in the first place to promote access – in those days from dissenting faiths whose members had been excluded from the Anglican monopolies of Oxford and Cambridge. To be head of the College at a time when we were able to give its founding tradition an extra dimension was both a proud and a humbling experience.

In my time at Mansfield the College grew in size. It also grew in self-confidence, while remaining true to its distinctive ethos and values. This was not due to me. It was due to the vitality and generosity of spirit of my colleagues – and by colleagues I mean the taught as well as the teachers.

These are times that try the souls of university teachers. A mean-minded managerialism pervades public policy towards higher education. The fundamental academic values of free enquiry, critical thinking and empathetic understanding have rarely been in greater danger. In Mansfield, at least, they flourish. That, above all, is why my time there will always glow in my memory.

Portraits of Principals

Mansfield's custom is for the Principal to sit for a portrait in the final year of their principalship. Portraits of all previous Heads of House hang high in the dining hall, where they keep a watchful eye over their successor. Consequently, the portraits displayed here do not include the current incumbent, Baroness Helena Kennedy, Principal 2011–. These paintings illustrate more than a century's evolution of both the nature of portraiture and also the way in which heads of Mansfield see themselves.

Andrew M. Fairbairn, 1886–1909, by Sir George Reid.

William B. Selbie, 1909–32, by Ernest Moore.

Donald Sykes, 1977–86, by Derek Fowler.

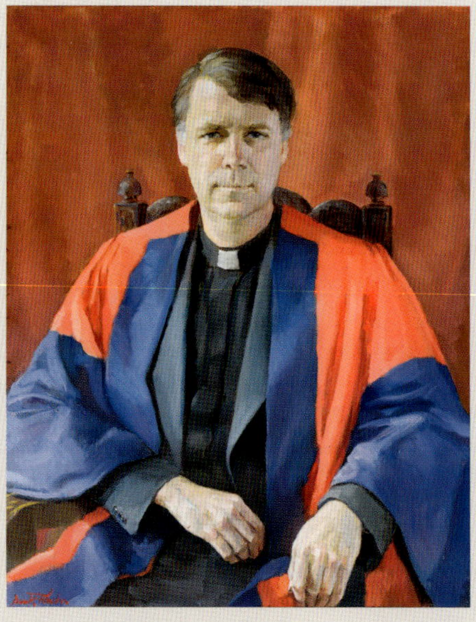

Jan Womer, 1986–8, by Derek Fowler.

Nathaniel Micklem, 1932–53, by Archie Utin.

John Marsh, 1953–70, by William Evens.

George Caird, 1970–7, by Derek Fowler.

Dennis Trevelyan, 1989–96, by Mark Alexander.

David Marquand, 1996–2002, by Richard Brazier.

Diana Walford, 2002–11, by Helen Masacz.

PART 5

Three Thematic Perspectives

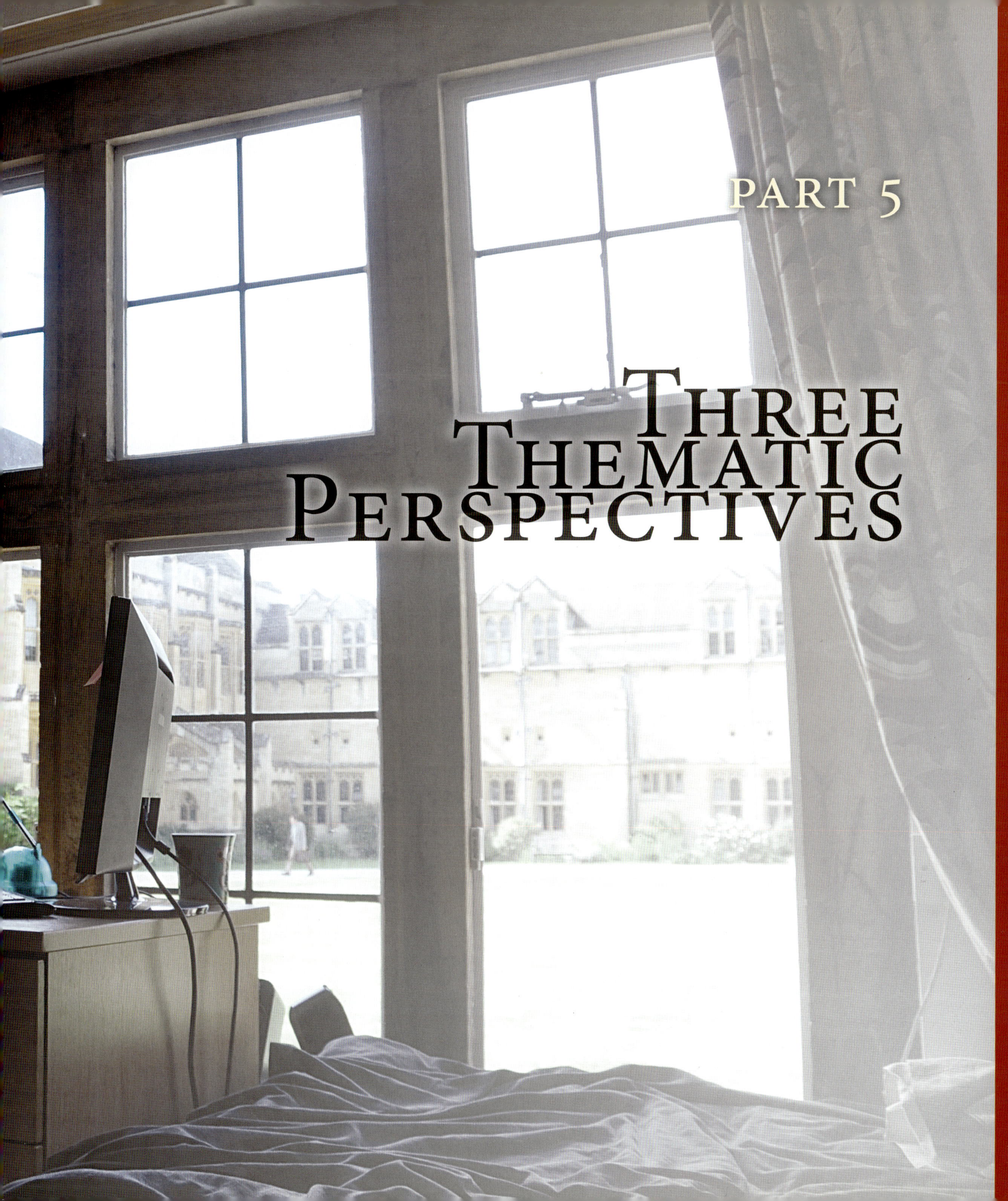

CONSUMING PASSIONS
Homographesis
VOLATILE BODIES
MARJORIE GARBER VESTED INTERESTS
REWRITING ENGLISH
ORHAN PAMUK THE BLACK BOOK
caribbean

English Language and Literature at Mansfield

Ros Ballaster

The University convention of describing academic study as 'reading' a subject is nowhere more aptly applied than to the subject of English. Decades of Mansfield students in English will attest that the undergraduate and graduate courses provide a strenuous experience of disciplined and extensive reading. But it is also an experience of discussion and exchange with their peers as well as their tutors.

When I meet graduates who studied English at Mansfield they recall a period of intense communion with books – and books in their many varieties and shapes. In *Areopagitica: A Speech for the Liberty of Unlicensed Printing to the Parliament of England* (1644), John Milton tells us that 'whatever thing we hear or see, sitting, walking, travelling, or conversing, may be fitly called our book'. 'Many a man lives a burden to the earth'; Milton continues, 'but a good book is the precious life-blood of a master spirit, embalmed and treasured up on purpose to a life beyond life.'

Some 40 years before Milton published his famous tract, Francis Bacon exhorted his readers: 'For friends … do but look

Previous pages: A student room overlooking the quad.

Left: Ros Ballaster, Tutor in English, making the most of limited space.

upon good Books: they are true friends, that will neither flatter nor dissemble' (*The Advancement of Learning*, 1605). English graduates form friendships with books and, we hope, carry on a lifelong relationship with writing and reading after they leave Oxford. And they also form friendships through books that survive long after the shiver of fear recalling an essay crisis or stepping into examination schools for finals assessment or a viva.

I was myself a graduate of an Oxford college in English, so I know that every student has a 'tutorial story'. Mine concerns a refined tutor trained firmly in the aesthetic school of Helen Gardner, whose only response to my undergraduate attempts to grapple in the early 1980s with the new theories of deconstruction, Marxism and feminism informing English studies with reference to the poetry of John Keats was to bring her fingertips together, fix her gaze on a patch of wall above my head and murmur softly, 'I think not, my dear'. I have not attempted here to collect such stories but rather to provide a brief sense of the changing nature of studying English at Mansfield since its first tutors were appointed on a part-time basis in 1960: Malcolm Parke and Stephen Wall. I have had the privilege of meeting every one of those tutors at some point in my own career.

Malcolm Parke, who also held a post at University College, ran a seminar for graduate research students. Every year he imparted the invaluable advice to record every book reference on a file card, and I still retain the three tin boxes that served me so well in the final writing up of my doctoral thesis. Stephen Wall – critic of the Victorian novel, director, and editor of the still-flourishing Oxford journal *Essays in Criticism*, whose death in 2010 we record with great sadness – came to visit the College

Lucinda Rumsey, Senior Tutor and Fellow in Early English Literature, in the middle of a tutorial.

shortly after my appointment to discuss the establishment of a fund at the College to support theatre research, kindly donated by the trustees of the estate of a former student, John Hodgson. John Hodgson (who took his degree as a mature student from 1960 to 1963) formed a group of players at Mansfield, and the chaplain gave agreement that plays could be staged in the College chapel. These were always popular and well attended, and the tradition continues.

Another distinguished director who graduated from Mansfield in the first year of my appointment (1994), Abigail Anderson, brought a Hallowe'en production of Gothic readings to Mansfield chapel. A group of undergraduate students worked with Abigail and myself to develop a theatrical performance and lecture about *The Arabian Nights*, given in the chapel to visitors at the annual summer event of 2008.

The enthusiasm for Milton is shared by many of Mansfield's tutors. John Creaser, Mansfield's first full Fellow in English (1966–85), is now an Emeritus Fellow. John's essay of 2007, '"Service is perfect freedom": Paradox and Prosodic Style in *Paradise Lost*' in *The Review of English Studies*, was awarded the James Holly Hanford Prize by the Milton Society of America for the most distinguished essay on Milton published in 2007.

Professor Mason Lowance, an alumnus of Mansfield who studied with John Creaser and continues to meet with him when he visits the College, is now at the University of Massachusetts. He teaches and publishes on American literature with a special interest in anti-slavery debates and writings. He has also endowed prizes to recognise distinguished second-year tutorial work and final examination performances among our English cohort.

NO FOOD OR DRINK

'A few years after leaving Mansfield I was back in Oxford, and I bumped into one of my tutors. "Well", he asked, "was it all worth it in the end?" "Worth it?" I said, "It transformed my life." He seemed genuinely surprised by my reply, and genuinely pleased. I came up to Mansfield in the autumn of 1984, to read English. I imagine it is the same for everyone arriving at Mansfield for the first time. The beauty of Champneys' buildings, and the expansive open quad, meeting tutorial partners, receiving reading lists, exploring the town. In those first weeks, nothing about Oxford failed to match up to my dream. I loved reading English, and the experience has remained with me ever since.'

Donald Macdonald – *1984, English*

I came to Mansfield in 1993, succeeding Kate Flint, Mansfield's first female Tutorial Fellow, who had moved to a University lectureship at Linacre (and subsequently to a chair at Rutgers, New Jersey). I have worked with Lucinda Rumsey, College Fellow in Early English literature and now Senior Tutor of the College, in friendship and with a shared commitment to open access and ongoing development of the quality of learning and teaching in our subject. That commitment has been recently renewed and refreshed with the appointment in 2009 of Michèle Mendelssohn as a second joint University and College Fellow in English. Michèle's expertise in 19th-century English and American literature, and research interest in transatlanticism, means that at the end of the first decade of the 21st century Mansfield College has a teaching establishment in English that encompasses the entire historical range (so much prized) of the Oxford undergraduate syllabus.

We also feel very proud of our expansion through the admission of graduate students to the College. There are undergraduates who now hold doctoral degrees undertaken at Mansfield, and are providing classes and tutorials to our incoming students.

The College can look back on its history and anticipate its future in teaching English with great pride. I conclude by quoting the words of a favourite 18th-century author, Laurence Sterne (for many students his *Tristram Shandy* probably stands with Milton's *Paradise Lost* as the most memorable and arduous of reads undertaken in the course of the undergraduate degree). In one of his letters (CXXX), Sterne speaks eloquently of conversing through books with others, surely the main satisfaction of one's time in an Oxford college, no matter how brief or extended:

> I often derive a peculiar satisfaction in conversing with the ancient and modern dead, – who yet live and speak excellently in their works. My neighbours think me often alone, – and yet at such times I am in company with more than five hundred mutes – each of whom, at my pleasure, communicates his ideas to me by dumb signs – quite as intelligently as any person living can do by uttering of words.

1133
Pro Motorsport® SPEEDSCOTLAND.COM
MR Turbo
I/BFS
DIGATRON

Materials Science at Mansfield

John Sykes

Over the last two decades the physical sciences have at last joined the mix of subjects in the College. Earlier attempts to take metallurgists (and chemists too) had fizzled out in the 1970s. It began with the election of Norman Booth, a nuclear physicist, and myself, a metallurgist, to supernumerary fellowships in 1987. My post was linked to a new engineering course called Electronic and Structural Materials Engineering, to be taught by the Departments of Engineering and of Metallurgy and Science of Materials. (In those days 'Materials Science' was rejected by the University as ungrammatical.) John Harding, our engineering Fellow, was eager for Mansfield to be involved with this new course, as it fitted with his research interests. It gave him the bonus, at a time when our student numbers were tightly regulated by the University, of two additional student places each year to help grow the cohort of engineers in the College.

Of course, it was not long (two years) before the College started to recruit undergraduates in both physics and metallurgy, and the numbers of scientists and engineers in the College began

Rick Pearson (1988, Engineering Science) attempts a world land-speed record in the summer of 2011 at the Bonneville Salt Flats in Utah.

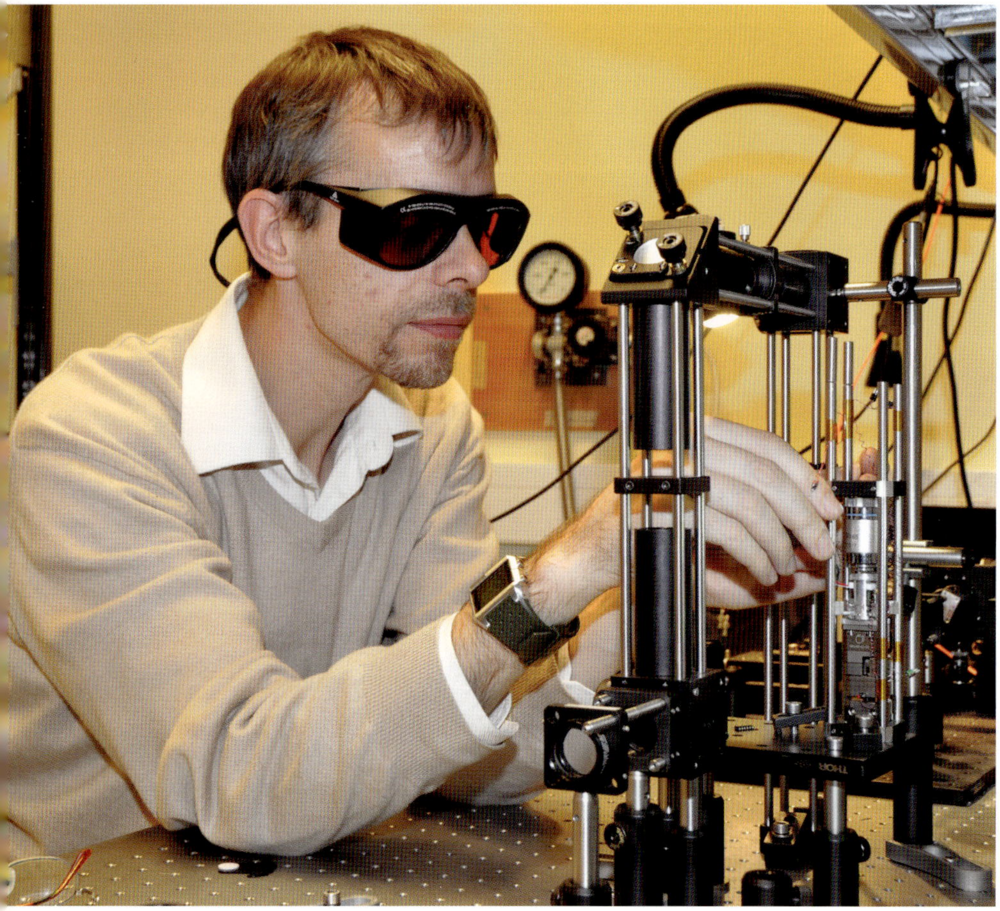

Jason Smith, Tutorial Fellow in Materials Science, in his lab.

John Sykes, Emeritus Professor of Materials.

to increase year by year. Initially, both subjects took just one pair of students, and, given the uncertainties in the admissions process, some years a fresher would arrive to find they were the only student in his or her subject. The physics course is always heavily oversubscribed, and numbers have grown steadily, but in materials science there has been a constant need to sell the subject to schools where it is not a main subject in the curriculum. Nevertheless, departmental numbers are now rising in a healthy way, and when we took the opportunity of sponsorship from Hewlett Packard to appoint Jason Smith, who had read physics at Wadham, as a second Tutorial Fellow, we increased the quota to four, then five.

But there have been setbacks along the way. One year (1993), after steady growth, there was a sudden drop in overall numbers to 14, and Sonia Matossian found herself the lone materials fresher in the College and one of only two women on the course.

Recruitment also proved a problem for electronic and structural materials engineering. The places were not ring-fenced, and stronger candidates for engineering science kept applicants out. It was clear from UCAS application forms that schools didn't understand what the course was about, and the title was changed to engineering and materials, but numbers still remained low, so eventually the University's last EMS student graduated recently when the course was finally closed. It was an ambitious course, aiming to inculcate

Science students at Mansfield may be found in the college library…

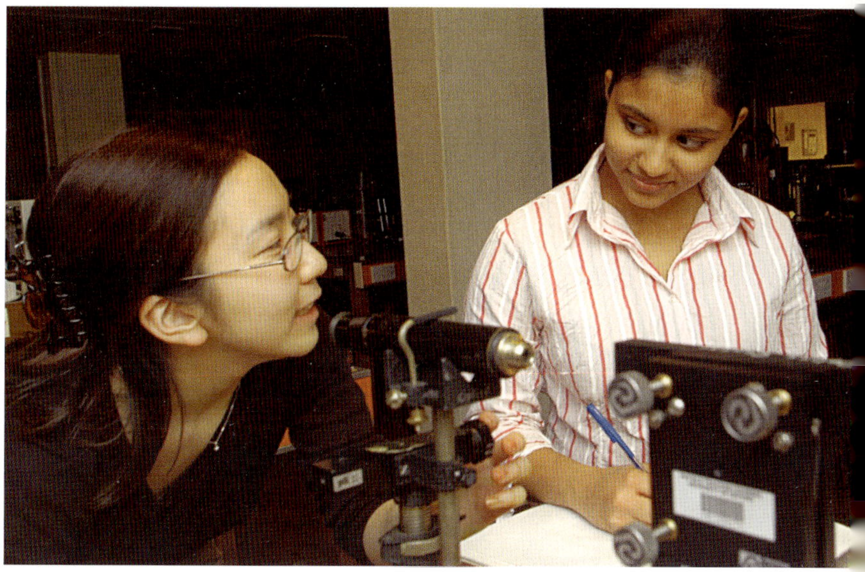

…or in the laboratory.

the design skills of the engineer and the scientific understanding and curiosity of the materials scientist, so that the would-be materials engineers were kept busy. We are now seeing the fruits of that concept as our graduates make successful careers in industry. One recently took on the post of project manager in composite structures at McLaren, the Formula 1 constructors, and another, Rick Pearson, made an attempt on a world land-speed record in the summer of 2011 at Bonneville Salt Flats, as well as having a successful career in finance. (He is sponsoring a Mansfield engineer to join his team.)

The arrival of scientists changed the pattern of student life, for their study did not revolve around reading and the weekly tutorial essay. Their days were filled with lectures that often began at 9.00 and many hours of practical work in laboratories that then had to be carefully written up. One of the metallurgists told me that Richard Underhill's practicals book (he was one of our first pair, and he won the Institute of Materials prize in Finals) had become the essential study guide at Mansfield. Perhaps it still is. I wonder if anybody ever discovered that the technicians switch the labels on the metallography samples from time to time.

In the early years Glyn Taylor provided the teaching in mechanical properties – setting monster essays for tutorial work – and Mike Goringe from Pembroke, where I was already a tutor, taught materials physics and electronic properties. Nowadays materials teaching is organised as a team with Corpus Christi and Queen's, with four Fellows sharing the tutorials for around 40 students across the three colleges. The link began with Amanda Petford-Long at Corpus Christi (where physics had already started sharing teaching) and was expanded when Queen's appointed Keyna O'Reilly and began taking materials undergraduates rather than engineers. Pete Nellist replaced Amanda at Corpus when she moved to a post in Chicago. (Her son has just taken Part I Materials here.)

Jocelyn Bell Burnell, Professorial Fellow in Physics, is the discoverer of pulsars.

A computer simulation of a pulsar from NASA, showing lines of magnetic field and the powerful jets of radiation emitted from the poles.

Norman Booth was ably assisted from the outset with first year mathematics by Candadi Sukumar (now a Fellow at Wadham but still teaching for Mansfield). They were later joined by Caroline Fraser, a popular and energetic tutor who tragically died from malaria at Christ Church (where she was a lecturer) after a Christmas trip to South Africa. On Norman's retirement, the College appointed condensed matter physicist Stephen Blundell as the first physics Tutorial Fellow, and closely followed this with particle physicist, Steve Biller. Student numbers in physics at Mansfield went up to six a year, and the subject went from strength to strength.

The sciences have also played a major part in the growth of the Middle Common Room, with a steady flow of postgraduate students in both physics and materials, some home-grown at Mansfield, but many more from universities around the world. We are in an ideal location for the sciences.

The most eminent of our science Fellows is Jocelyn Bell Burnell, the discoverer of pulsars, who has become both a Dame and the President of the Institute of Physics during her time at the College. Her election to a fellowship was arranged when she joined the Department of Physics as a visiting professor. One new student was open-mouthed at the freshers' dinner to find himself sitting opposite Dame Jocelyn. 'We studied about her at school!' he whispered to his neighbour.

Most recently James Marrow, the new James Martin Professor of Energy Materials, has joined us from Manchester University as a Professorial Fellow, and on my retirement in 2010 Marina Galano became a Tutorial Fellow in materials.

Stephen Blundell and PhD students performing experiments using muons at a laboratory in Switzerland.

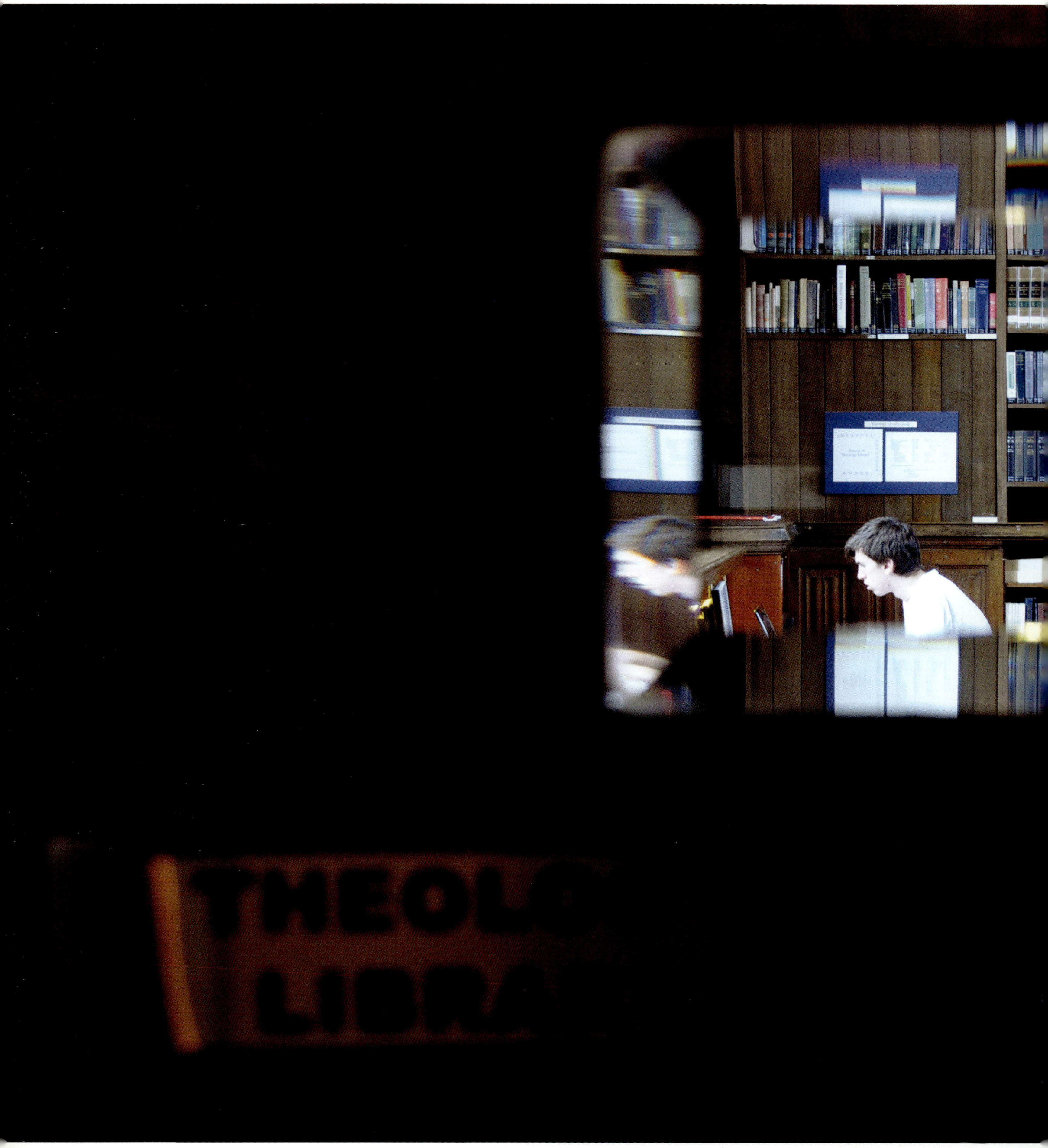
THEOL
LIBR

Theology and Religion at Mansfield in the 21st Century

Joel D.S. Rasmussen *and*
Tanya N. Stormo Rasmussen

In many respects reading theology at Mansfield in the 21st century has become decidedly different from the experience it was for most who took theology degrees here in the twentieth century. One indicator of this is the decision within the University to change the name of the Theology Faculty to the 'Faculty of Theology and Religion' (with effect from Michaelmas 2012), and this reflects reforms in the Faculty syllabus that build on Oxford's historic strengths in the study of Christianity, extending it to include the study of the world's other major religions. An even more proximate indicator of the transformation, however, was the graduation of Mansfield's final ministerial training candidate in 2009. That event marked the outcome of a decision by the United Reformed Church (URC) to consolidate its energies and resources in its four other colleges across Great Britain. In the wake of that decision, it is tempting to say that most current students who elect to study theology and religion at Mansfield do so for more purely academic reasons rather than vocational ones. But this

The Theology Library.

John Muddiman, Tutorial Fellow in New Testament Studies, in his room.

distinction would be too heavy-handed, and risks blinking past the fact that our best students – undergraduates and postgraduates – still conceive their academic work as a vocation in the highest sense: a calling to the life of the mind, to use Hannah Arendt's phrase. Of course, this doesn't mean that we are now primarily in the business of turning out the next generation of professional scholars of religion. Nor should it suggest that current students are uninterested in practical matters. It simply means they feel called to develop their own best possible understandings of the range of subjects that comes under the overall heading of 'Theology and Religion'.

It is this very broad range of subject areas that characterises the main difference between studying theology and religion at Mansfield today as compared to past times. Just a few years ago, when a member of the Mansfield Association learned that the College had recently appointed a new tutor with a specialism in 19th-century philosophical theology, the alumnus remarked: 'Well, there was no such thing as 19th-century theology when I was at Oxford!' Obviously, he hadn't graduated in the 18th century – it was simply that his experience of theology in Oxford was one that focused predominantly on biblical literature, and in which the historical papers concluded with the Ecumenical Council of Chalcedon in 451. Today, the options have grown to include not only modern Christian history, but also the social and intellectual histories of Judaism, Islam, Hinduism and Buddhism. Additional to that, papers in science and religion, sociology of religion and the psychology of religion are increasingly popular. Considering the fact that we also have students reading in the Joint School of Philosophy and Theology and now in the Joint School in Theology and Oriental Studies, then taken as a whole, today's crop of theology and religion students probably stands among the most liberally educated of all those who take humanities degrees.

In a number of ways Mansfield has taken a leading role in this broader vision for the study of theology and religion in the University. We've embraced this vision rather than shrinking from it, and this makes it an exciting time to be a part of a new chapter in the history of Mansfield College. To date, Mansfield is the only college with two Theology and Religion Faculty post-holders as Tutorial Fellows – John Muddiman in New Testament Studies and Joel Rasmussen in Philosophical Theology and Modern Religious

Tanya Stormo Rasmussen, ordained in the United Methodist Church in the United States, has been chaplain and Fellow of Mansfield since 2006.

John Muddiman meeting Pope Benedict XVI at the celebration of the 40th anniversary of Dei Verbum*, 2005.*

History – working alongside the lecturer in the study of religions, Peggy Morgan, and chaplain Fellow, Tanya Rasmussen. The recent appointment of David Lincicum to succeed John Muddiman as G. B. Caird Fellow in New Testament Theology in Michaelmas Term 2012 ensures that Mansfield is moving from strength to strength in a subject in which the College has historically been at the scholarly forefront.

With the transition in the religious life of the College having moved away from theological training of ordinands, chapel life in the College has also shifted. Today's semi-weekly worship services remain grounded in the Reformed tradition, and there is active encouragement for people of all religious traditions (or none) to view Mansfield's chapel as a place for them to engage in prayer, meditation and worship. Rooted in the conviction that the Holy Other is often encountered or revealed through music and the arts, free weekly recitals are offered at lunchtime on Wednesdays during term (under the coordination of John Oxlade, organist and director of music); the chapel has hosted an increasing number of plays and concerts; and more regular art exhibitions are in the works.

The topical symposium is a new initiative of the chaplaincy, providing an opportunity to explore the religious dimensions of various current issues in an informal setting. Feminism, the death of theatre, whether the Bible can 'be trusted', and the relationship between 'Sexuality, spirituality, and the whole person' are just a few of the popular topics we've engaged with. This weekly gathering nurtures community and understanding by offering an open and egalitarian forum to students, Fellows, staff and friends. Topics regularly range from the theological to the political, the cultural to the scientific, the ethical to the aesthetic (and anything in between). All explored over wine and cheese.

Times are changing, and understanding religion in a secular age is a difficult and important task. Mansfield College has long been at the forefront of critically exploring the religious issues of the day in deep conversation with the past – that, at least, has not changed. As Søren Kierkegaard once remarked, 'Life can only be understood backwards; but it must be lived forwards'. Theology and religion are the warp and woof of the historical life of this College, and it is a great honour and responsibility to be involved in helping to weave together an even fuller future for Mansfield.

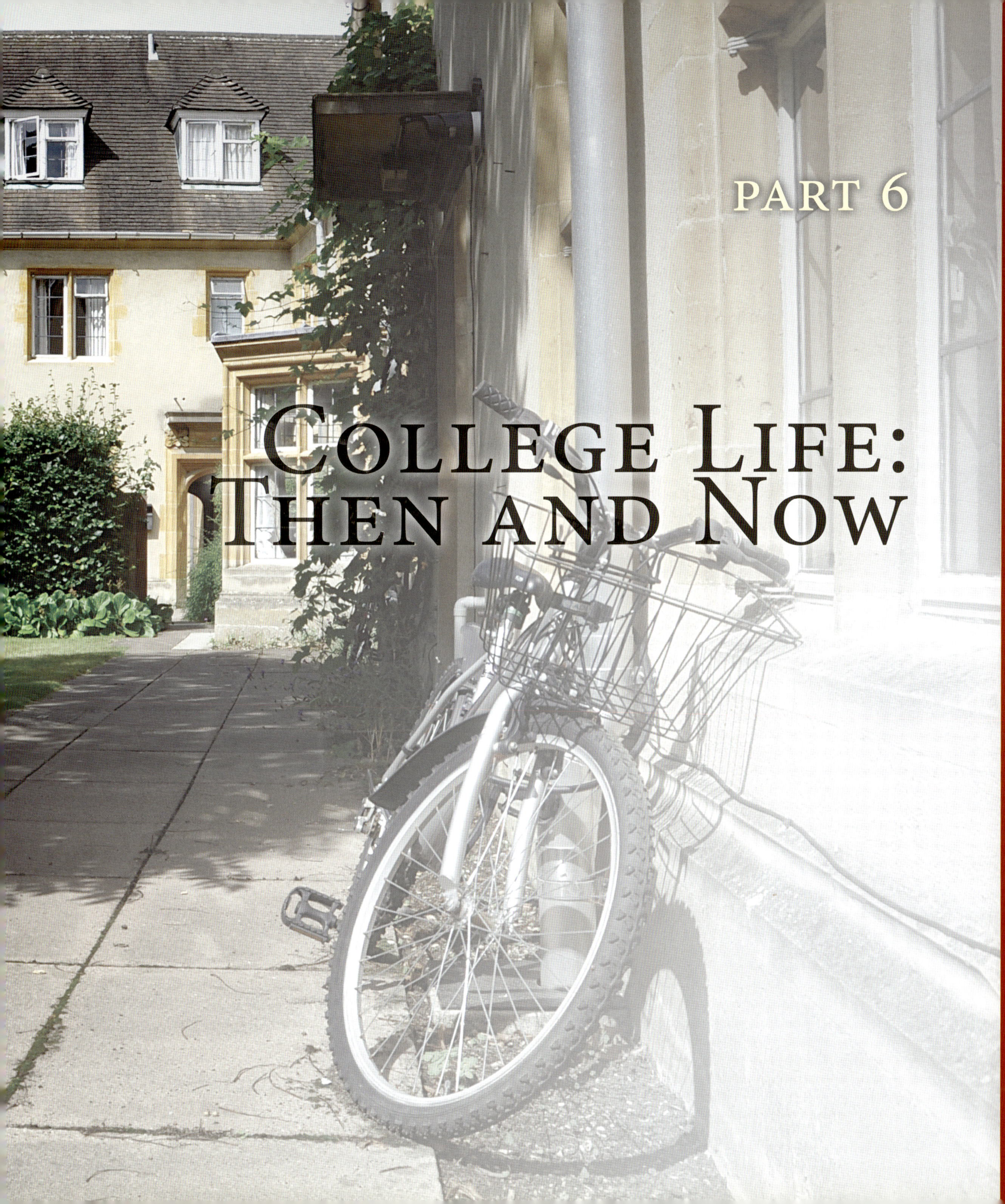

PART 6

COLLEGE LIFE: THEN AND NOW

DOLGOCH STATION
TALYLLYN RAILWAY
TOWYN MERIONETH WALES

Recollections of a Chaplain

Charles Brock

Coming to Mansfield in 1962 fresh from Harvard, I could hardly understand the local accent, let alone the customs, but I was determined. I rounded out my theological education by attending lectures by John Marsh and George Caird. I met C.H. Dodd and tried enthusiastically to engage him on his work, but he kept looking the other way. Donald Sykes offered to teach me Greek, but I gave up after the first session – it wasn't his fault as a nicer guy couldn't be found anywhere, and he actually liked Americans. I was a dumbo with languages – especially English.

John Marsh (J.M.) liked Americans too, at least for their money at a time when Mansfield was struggling. George Caird liked Canadians and didn't venture south of the border much. But he did have funny stories. George knew an ancient scholar during the McCarthy era who crossed the border at Niagara Falls when you had to vow not to overthrow the American government by force. The blighter wrote 'sole purpose of visit'. He got in then, but now there would be soldiers and black helicopters chasing him.

Previous pages: The back of the Rayson Building.

Left: Student room in the John Marsh Building, 1962.

Charles Brock, College chaplain 1965–98, preaching in the chapel.

My parents left us a VW mini-bus after they left Britain from a holiday in Europe, and I took the ordinands to various classes, especially at the psychiatric hospital where we had an afternoon each week on symptom recognition of mental problems. We needed that for our churches. We had a pushy Presbyterian psychiatrist who claimed that an old lady couldn't feel a needle when he put it into her hand. When he inserted it she almost jumped out the window, and it was hard to keep ourselves under control. He laughed so hard that his glasses dropped off. Those were the moments we loved.

Somehow, to everybody's amazement, I was appointed chaplain – solely by J.M., who didn't ask the other SCR members. Those were the days. I got the cold shoulder from some at first, and it didn't help that I had rather weird (for the British) ideas about what could happen in the chapel. After the first year J.M. said: 'Charles, when are you leaving?' I was too innocent to take that amiss and replied, 'Oh, I really like it here.' On I stayed until our first appointed secular Fellow Anthony Ogus pushed me into a fellowship. Luckily, I wasn't at that meeting, but I did feel my ears tingle. Anthony and I got along well (as I did with the first tranche of a very good bunch of seculars, including John Creaser, Mike Mahony, Michael Freeden and Tony Lemon), and with Carolyn I attended his Jewish wedding at Strasbourg. Anthony's brother was a doctor. His father didn't find it as amusing as I did that there was a doctor and lawyer in the family. Dan Cohn Sherbok, when a visiting scholar at Mansfield, said that when he was asked as a youngster whether he was going to be a doctor or a lawyer he answered by saying 'a rabbi'. The storekeeper said: 'Ach, not a job for a good Jewish boy.'

As SCR steward in charge of wine, snuff box and other essentials, I got on well with the downstairs staff. I was invited to conduct weddings for them from time to time. There were many characters, and the College steward Wally Buckingham will never be forgotten as long as Donald Sykes and I are around to tell stories about him. His height and ramrod body stoked fear in the undergraduates, and he could oust with ease SCR members, including myself, who hadn't signed in for dinner. He kept a formality of office, but when you had Wally and Beryl for dinner it was all wonderfully equal. Susan Keane , the veteran College scout, was still serving the SCR with total and loving commitment.

Matriculation 1966.

During the late 1960s we had our share of hippies, and one JCR president also helped with the organ for chapel services – mainly by laying his elbows on the keyboards. Another, named Sid, was a Texas rancher and also JCR president if my memory serves me correctly, and he walked Principal Dennis Trevelyan the entire length of Manhattan probably because he didn't want to hear about Mansfield's dire straits. But Sid did turn up at Commem for years on end, so he must have heard it there.

The Lutheran tutors in the SCR were mainly a charming bunch with good academic qualifications, and they often brought European visitors to dine. But the best times were the Friday guest nights, and I tried to get to most of them. I sat next to some interesting people from academia, churches and government. On one occasion a nice woman asked me how we taught chemistry in the States. I didn't know too much about that, but the wine was good and I sallied forth. It wasn't until the next day I learned that she had just won the Nobel Prize in chemistry.

I got to know Iris Murdoch at guest night as well, and subsequently she paid a visit to my WEA class on 'Love and Evil in Contemporary Literature', which covered about everything as long as it was less than 200 pages for the week's read. She asked me some rather personal questions, on which again I was happy to hold forth. When I asked her how she wrote her books, she said: 'Oh, I meet some people and put them together in my mind with others, and out comes a story. I have no idea how it is going to end. It takes me about 18 months from start to finish.' Exactly 18 months later I got her latest novel in the mail from her – but it couldn't have been about me. Though he was a chaplain, tutor, interested in Freudian theory and loved Oxford, he was a thoroughly rotten person.

Ah, Oxford. *Quo vadis?* How we miss thee!

Music at Mansfield

Mansfield College enjoys a reputation for the performance of music. For many years this activity was under the direction of Carolyn Brock (conductor of the City of Oxford Choir) and more recently it has continued under John Oxlade, the current director of music and recently elected an Honorary Fellow of the College. This builds on a long and illustrious tradition, which includes musicians such as Albert Schweitzer, Alec Rowley and the composer and musicologist Erik Routley, a former Mansfield student who became chaplain from 1948–59. The chapel contains a historic three-manual organ built by Vowles of Bristol in 1890 and left virtually without modern modification in its original state. As the result of a generous bequest a fine grand piano was bought for the chapel. In 2007 a series of lunchtime recitals was launched and these are now a regular feature of chapel life, as well as termly concerts by the chapel choir who also sing at the Wednesday evening services during Term. The choir has recently performed a wide range of works, including Rossini's *Petite Messe Solennelle*, Schubert's *Deutsche Messe*, Bellini's *Gloria*, Faure's *Requiem*, Vaughan Williams' *Serenade to Music*, Bach's *St John Passion*, Stainer's *Crucifixion* and Elgar's setting of *For the Fallen*.

Students perform in a lunchtime recital in the chapel.

Paul Crossley, international concert pianist, was discovered while an undergraduate at Mansfield by Olivier Messiaen and his wife Yvonne Loriod in 1967.

From Mansfield to Messiaen – Paul Crossley

It would be utterly impossible to overstate the importance of Mansfield in my life, and yet I only arrived there by chance. My father, who had died when I was very young, had been to Sidney Sussex College, Cambridge, and it was assumed I would go there too. As luck would have it, a sudden and unexpected change of headmaster at my school (an Oxford, rather than a Cambridge man) pointed me in the direction of Mansfield, 'somewhere I think you might be very happy, and very successful,' he said. Well, well!

My school, Silcoates, Wakefield, was, like Mansfield, a Congregationalist foundation, and its life very much centred on the chapel of which I was organist. So, when I arrived in Mansfield I was immediately appointed organ scholar (though the College had never had one before), and I used the small stipend to finance monthly piano lessons with (the now-legendary) Fanny Waterman in Leeds. After a time, John Marsh asked me how they were going, and I had to admit that I'd stopped them because I had run out of money. 'Oh no you don't,' he said. 'The College will take care of everything as long as you are here.' This was the first, but the most essential, of the several acts of 'enlightened generosity' that were to come my way. Those three years of piano study were the solid foundation for everything that was to follow.

School excursions were few and far between, but when I was about 16 I was taken to a performance of Messiaen's great organ piece 'La Nativité du Seigneur' (it was actually the first live concert I had ever been to), and I was 'hooked'. I knew this was my music. I bought the score and tried to hear as much of his music as I could – not at all easy in those days – but, by the time of Mansfield I knew quite a lot. In the long vacation immediately after my finals, there was a festival of his music in London and in Oxford, and the organiser of that, hearing of my extreme devotion to his music, asked if I would stay on and help. As it happened, most of the players were 'billeted' in Mansfield, so my piano practice (I was still having lessons with Fanny Waterman) in the JCR was almost impossible. I knew the stage manager of the Oxford Playhouse, where some concerts were taking place, who suggested to me that I could use the gorgeous Steinway when nobody else was there. Accordingly, one morning, very early, I was practising a Mozart piano concerto when – suddenly – from behind the safety curtain I was joined by the orchestral accompaniment on an upright piano. Of course, I stopped at once, and who should appear but

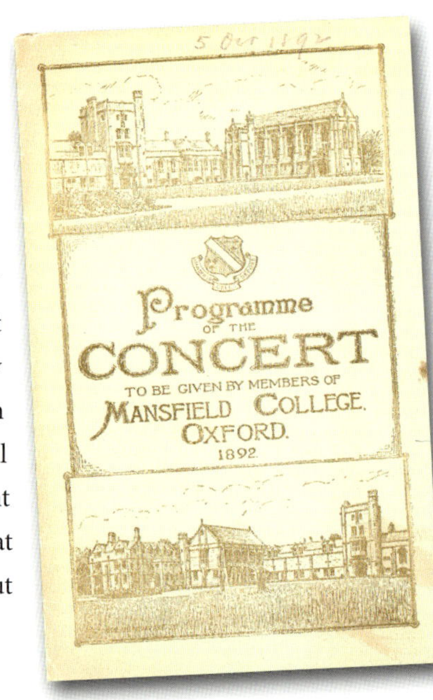

The chapel choir.

Messiaen and his wife, the pianist Yvonne Loriod. They asked me about myself, how had I learned to play 'so wonderfully', and what I was planning to do. I said I wasn't at all sure. 'Oh, we are,' they said. 'Come to Paris to study with us.' After I had picked myself up, I realised I couldn't see how this was possible – particularly financially. At a concert that evening I told my story to a prominent music critic, who advised me to contact the French cultural attaché and apply for a French government scholarship. I did – the next day – but was told that all had been awarded earlier in the year and that I should try again the following year. One week later I received a telephone call from the French embassy: 'Someone who had a scholarship now can't go – if you can be in Paris next week, it's yours.' And the rest is history – or not quite. Many years later, well into my career, I met the cultural attaché in Paris, and we reminisced about what had happened. 'Oh, it wasn't an accident,' she told me. 'We were all so intrigued by the Messiaens discovering you that Paris made an extra scholarship especially for you.'

College Sports

Mansfield is fortunate to share the fine Merton sports grounds which are located just eight minutes' walk from the College, behind St Catherine's College. Tennis and squash courts are available on the same site. The size of Mansfield's main quad makes for one of the best croquet lawns in the University and there is a much-used snooker table and equally popular dartboard.

Above: The 1899 Mansfield football team.

Above right: The Mansfield tennis team, 1966.

Right: The Mansfield cricket XI, 2011.

For many sports, Mansfield teams, or teams formed jointly with Merton, play in the inter-college 'cuppers' competitions, but there are many friendly matches too. Sport is a great way to get to know people at other colleges and Mansfield's small size makes

Left: *Eights Week: The Mansfield Women's 1st VIII, 2011.*

Below: *The 1987 Oxford and Cambridge Boat Race: OUBC President and Captain of the Blue boat, Donald Macdonald stands to celebrate his Oxford crew's epic victory.*

sport very accessible. All who want to play are very welcome and everyone can find a game at some level. And if your sport is one in which we do not regularly compete, find some like-minded people and start a team (when this happened in basketball we won cuppers!).

The Boat Race Mutiny – Donald Macdonald

It is 25 years since the Oxford Boat Race Mutiny. At the time, in the winter of 1987, it was a grim battle for survival – my own and the integrity of a 158-year-old amateur institution. In the end we prevailed and went on to win our race against Cambridge in dramatic style and against all the odds. It clearly struck a chord at the time, because the following year the story became a bestselling book, *True Blue*, and a little later a film of the same name, starring Dominic West, was made.

In Oxford the story has acquired an almost cult status within the college rowing community. Succeeding generations of crews have sat down together before Torpids and Eights to watch *True Blue* and get focused for their racing. Over the years I've been asked to recount the story to audiences from corporations to colleges and even inside a prison.

The story endures because it captures so well universal themes with which all of us can readily identify. Life throws up unexpected challenges, and all of us will make mistakes. The true test, however, is how we respond. *True Blue* is about how we can find ways to win in the face of adversity.

I've often wondered how things would have been had I been a student at a college other than Mansfield. At the height of the conflict the pressures were enormous. There was little escape from the relentless attention of journalists, disaffected oarsmen and even on occasion the University proctors. Throughout it all Mansfield remained steadfast, supportive and concerned for my welfare, none of which will come as a surprise to many of you reading this.

The Boat Race Mutiny was a defining event in my life, and over the course of the last quarter of a century the story has taken its place in the history and mythology of Mansfield. It's become part of the fabric of my life, inextricably woven with Mansfield into the memory of my time at Oxford.

A Soupçon of Mansfield

It may be a slight exaggeration to suggest that the quality of Mansfield soups is what holds the College together, but there is no denying their pulling power. They would grace any top-class restaurant, and make both lunch and dinner a delectable experience. Lynn Partridge, Food & Beverage Manager, describes their inspiration:

> As a child of post-war austerity, soup played a major part in my childhood. Soup used to be the main part of the evening meal, mostly vegetarian. My mother was a very good cook and some of my ideas and recipes come from her.
>
> All the chefs at Mansfield have input about which soups we try out and over the years we have found a few favourites! I think the most popular one is roasted butternut squash, chilli and coconut. This soup came about when we had a glut of butternut squash given to me by a neighbour; we tried several variations and decided on the one we use today.

College Reflections

'I used to love walking up and down Mansfield road, and greeting every other person that I passed. Mansfield was a real community, and everyone did seem to know each other, to the surprise of colleagues from other colleges.'

TRACY BAKER (NEE HART) – *1998, MATHEMATICS*

'Because the College was so small – the JCR comprised about 100 undergraduates, the MCR another 20 or so ordinands, many from overseas – there wasn't enough space for cliques and factions. It was one of the friendliest, most open colleges of its time.'

PETER VICKERS – *1979, HISTORY*

The Arrival: freshers settle into Mansfield.

Freshers' event: signing up for a society.

Undergraduate teaching continues to be carried out in tutorials, here with Paul Lodge, Tutorial Fellow in Philosophy.

Summer Ball and a floodlit college.

A JCR meeting: students listen and discuss.

'There were rules to be followed – or got round. Visitors were not allowed in the morning or after 10pm in my first year, thankfully times which were more relaxed by the final year. Unless you had an exeat you had to be back in College before midnight or run the gauntlet of patrolling Proctors with their bowler-hatted 'bulldogs'. A much greater risk, however, was being caught returning after midnight by the Principal, John Marsh, who would sometimes be walking his dog in the early hours. And of course you were not allowed to have visitors staying in your room overnight and it was important not to be caught if you did, since before breakfast there would be a knock on your door and Wally Buckingham, the College Steward, would come in and open your curtains with a cheery 'Good morning, Sir'. Luckily he never checked the wardrobe.'

Bob Porrer – 1963, *Modern Languages*

'It is impossible to define what my time at Mansfield did for me. The experience is seared into my memory and the wonderful stories of my three years are far too numerous to recall. I am grateful for the friends I made and for all that I learned. The man I learned most from was the man who changed my life – and the lives of many others: Dr Michael Freeden. However, the brief encounter I look back on oddly took place 20 years after my departure from Oxford. It says so much about the man who gave birth to PPE at Mansfield, as well as his incalculable contribution to the wider academic community and beyond.

I have spent my career in investment banking, at Merrill Lynch. A few years ago I was searching for a young, smart addition to my team and I interviewed Tom Morgan, a graduate from Teddy Hall. When I told him I had studied PPE at Mansfield in the early 1980s, the conversation changed. He asked me if Dr Freeden had taught me when I was there. I nodded, yes, and told him how much he meant to me. In one memorable movement of his upper body, Tom hauled himself up in his seat and raised his outstretched arms. He tossed his head back and declared, almost operatically 'Plato! … Aristotle!! … Freeden!!! I hired him on the spot.'

RICHARD KLEIN – *1982, PPE*

Michaelmas Term: Matriculation and calling the register before setting off for the Sheldonian.

'The day I walked through the gates of Mansfield was one of the most magical days of my life. I was warmly welcomed immediately by an undergraduate who politely enquired whether I needed any help. I nervously explained that I was looking for a Dr Freeden (who I understood was in charge of an ILEA scheme to help under-privileged children from inner London, on an entry scheme which by-passed the formal exam process).

I'd been interviewed by another college and knew I had not been offered a place. A working-class girl from Streatham, from a Catholic Comprehensive school and a single-parent family – I felt incongruous, as if I'd walked into George Orwell's A Clergyman's Daughter. *Dr Freeden listened and offered a simple solution. Apply. Choose the college you want and make an application. And so I did. I applied to Mansfield, the most welcoming place I'd encountered at Oxford so far.*

My three years studying PPE at Mansfield College were and still remain the most personally rewarding of my life. I feel a deep gratitude for the opportunity I was given to explore my passion for learning in such a wonderful environment.'

MARIAN BUCKLEY – *1985, PPE*

The Matriculation ceremony in the Sheldonian.

Relaxing in the bar, at snooker and table football.

'The first word that comes to mind when thinking back on my year as a visiting student at Mansfield College from 2007–8 is "whirlwind". From that first trip to the Turf with the freshers to the last formal dinner held for the VSPs at the end of Trinity, I always felt at home within the Mansfield community.'

Amanda Stellato – *2007, visiting student*

The owl and Erasmus the pussycat.

'There were only around 50 students in our intake and yet undergraduates from other colleges would remark not just on how friendly Mansfield seemed, how relaxed we all were, but how we seemed to pop up all over town, over-represented in social clubs, doing well on the river and the sports fields, and generally having a very good time!'

Sarah Harkness – *1980, PPE*

'I remember my time at Mansfield fondly. I thoroughly enjoyed reading English, studying in the Bodleian, the tutorial system and the friendships.'

Philip Rattle – *1984, English*

Trinity Term: Finals and degree ceremonies.

'It was well over a year since we'd last stood on the quad feeling slightly awkward in our sub fusc, preparing ourselves for the trip to the Exam Schools. Now, there were smiles and laughter all round, as we were reunited to finally celebrate making it through university. We raced to the Exam Schools, pausing only for photos under the Bridge of Sighs. The Graduation ceremony then began, and I think we all felt quite proud as the Vice-Chancellor impressed upon us the achievements that were being celebrated, and how, in graduating from this university, we were joining the ranks of thousands of similarly-robed graduands that had gone before us over the centuries.'

Lucy May – *2006, English*

List of Subscribers

This book was supported by the generosity of the subscribers listed below. Apart from dates of service, dates given are those of matriculation to the University.

Bashir Ahmed 1979
Stacy Albanese 1987
David Allen 1953
The Revd Albert E. Alspach 1963
Dr Pamela Sue Anderson 1979
Jonathan Arkush 1973
Catherine E. Ashford 1999
David J. Bailey 1984
Sara Bainbridge 2007
Richard Baker 1980
Tracy Baker (née Hart) 1998
Adrian Barlow 2000
J.W.E. Barnard 2007
Dr Crawford F. Barnett Jr 1962
Susannah Bartholomew
William Bartholomew
Richard Bazzaz 2002
The Revd Geoffrey E. Beck 1942
John Bell 1970
Thomas F. Best 1965
Leoni Betts 2001
Christopher Birrell 1973
Liane Black
Sidney Blankenship 1967
Revd Robert J. Blows 1958
Jamie Blythin 2006
Clayton Bond 2000
Derek Bond 1973
Richard Bonshek 1968
Timothy Booth 1978
Sylvia Boullé
Tim Bower and Helen Bower (née Fraser) 1979
Andrew Bradley 1979
Matthew Breitfelder 1993
Clive Brill 1980
Joel Michael Brookes 1992
Nicholas Broomfield 2006
Imogen Buchan 2010
Marian Buckley 1985
Michael Burton 1971
Daniel Butchart-Kuhlmann 2006
Sally Caless 2000
Leighton Cardwell 2002
Katherine Louise Carpenter 1999
Peter Carroll 1971
Frederick L Chenery 1965
Shin Chiba 1974
A.C. McHugh de Clare 1997
Professor Howard Clark **Fellow 2002–11**
Revd Malcolm Clarke 1970
Revd Timothy N. Clarke 1992
Finbar Clenaghan 1994
David Clyde 1997
David Collins 1974
Kate Compston 1969
Douglas R. Connor 1971
2Lt R.A. Cooper 2005
Nigel Cowmeadow 1980
John Creaser 1961; **Emeritus Fellow**
John Croasdale 1983
Andrew Croxson 1992
Sian Croxson 1991
Robert Cumberland 2000
Charlotte Cummins 1996
Daniel G. Currell 1992
Tom Cutler 1991
Stephen Davies 1999
Graham Davis 1982
Andrew Daykin 1963
P.J. Dean
James Dingemans 1983
Adam Andrew Dmytriw 2009
Richard L. Dodds 1957
Garry Dore **Head Porter 2012–**
J. Hugh Dorrell 1966
Eleanor Doyle (née Burn) 1998
Christian Dubé 2006
Elaine Dunn 1990
Michaela Durrant 1997
Mr and Mrs S. Dyson
Debbie Edwards (née Cozens) 1997
Marcus Edwards 2000
Dr Philip G. Engstrom
David M. Evans 1978
Elizabeth Evans 2008
William Evans 1996
D.A.J. Falkner 1997
Hugo Fearon 2010
Emily L. Feltham 2009
Stuart Ferguson 1993
Edward J. Finch 2008
Jerry Folk 1963
Roy Foster 1964
Tom Foster 2005
Peter Froebel 1966
Stepen M. Gaskell
Revd Theodore Gill 1976
Christopher Mark Glover 1994
Jenni Goodchild
John Greenland 1960
John Gregory and Rachel Gregory (née Adcock) 1982
Becky Griffiths 1998
Revd Tony Groom 1959
David Gulliver 1970
Melanie Hah 2007
Adrian C. Hall 1964
Sarah Harkness 1980
Peter Harrison-Evans 2010
Giles E. Harrison 1986
Ian Harrison 1966
David and Victoria Hartwell 2002
Marcus Haywood 1996

Jeff Hearn **1965**
Nicholas Hedley **1971**
Yang-Wahn Hew **1997**
Glenn S. Holland **1979**
Oliver Holloway **2008**
Michael Holyoake **1985**
Joseph Hone **2008**
James Hopkins **1978**
The Revd Michael Hopkins **1998**
Richard Hornby **1991**
Christopher Hoskin **1994**
Revd Dr Walter J. Houston **1964; Chaplain Fellow 2000–7**
Ian Howard **1977**
Rolf Howarth **1982**
Revd Dr Christopher Hucker **1998**
Fisher Humphreys **1965**
Brian Hunt **1978**
Nicola F. Ivory **2003**
Paul 'Jacko' Jackson **1992**
David M. James **1981**
Douglas Jeffery **1985**
Chris Jenkins **1977**
Alma Jenner **Librarian 1976–2011**
Alexandra Jezeph **2004**
Darin Johnson **1996**
Kate Johnson **2005**
Peter M. Johnson FRSA **1967**
Graeme A. Jones
Mark Gary Jones **1981**
Revd Dr Peter C. Jupp and Judge Elisabeth Jupp **1966**
Josephine Kahn **2010**
David Kell **1978**
Molly Kenyon **1980**
Robin Ketteridge **1984**
Revd John Key **1960**
Lee Kidd **1972**
Clive and Margaret King **1962**
Joanne King **1987**
Martin Kirkby **1975**
Maureen Klebanov **1959 (LMH)**
Richard Klein **1982**
The Revd Canon Arnold W Klukas **1970**
Michael Kudera **1993**
Andrew Lambert **1991**
Robert Lee **2007**
Anthony Lemon **1965; Fellow 1969–2010**
Peter Lerner **1966**
Malcolm Levi **1967**
Chris Lewis **1993**
Harrie M. Leyten **1973**
Charles Linaker **1975**
John J. Lipsey II **1987**
Liz and John Llewellyn-Lloyd **1980 and 1978**
Keith Lock **1965**
John S. Lombard **2001**
Revd Dr Roy Long **1967**
Ellen Loughnan **1992**
D.E. Lugton
Anthony Lunch **1964**
Eric Lund **1972**
John S.M. Lysons **1979**
Revd Cecil Macaulay **1986**
Donald H.M. Macdonald **1984**
Revd Peter John Mackriell **1982**
Julian Macro **1965**
Carol Mahony-Greatorex
In memory of Dr Michael Mahony
Steve Mann **1981**
Michael Margolis **1995**
Lucy Margolius (née Reed) **1995**
David Marquand **Principal 1996–2002**
Anthony R. Martin **1977**
Nick Mason **1958**
Barry Mawby **Head Porter 2007–12**
Beth McCarthy **2008**
Kerin McCauley **2008**
Catherine McClen **1988**
Robert O. McCracken **2002**
Revd Iain McDonald **1994**
Paul McEvoy MBE **1983**
Marian McKean (née Thorpe) **1950**
Helen McKenzie **2004**
Revd Dr Ian N. McPherson **1960**
Revd Professor Samuel J. Mikolaski **1956**
Brian Millar **1986**
Dana N. Mills **2008**
Edward Mishambi **2004**
Robert B. Mison **1984**
Katie Moore **2003**
Peggy Morgan **Lecturer 1992–**
Edward and Carolyn Bryce Morris **1995**
Richard T. Morrison **1987**
Elizabeth Ethun Moseley **2003**
Gerald C. Moule **2004**
J.B. Muddiman **1965; Fellow 1990–2012**
Ian 'Nellie' Neville **1974**
Dr Edward Newbold **1988**
Revd Dr Donald W. Norwood **1959**
V.R. O'Connell **1959**
Abigail Cinader Olson **1987**
David Parry **1965**
Capt Matthew Paterson **2003**
Nick Pattinson **1966**
Gina Pattisson Beloff **1995**
Steven Paul **1977**
Joseph A. Petriello **2000**
David A. Pickering **1986**
Isobel Plant **2008**
Stephen Pollard **1985**
Prashant Popat QC **1987**
Robert Porrer **1963**
Mrs C.C. Pot-Mees
The Revd Daphne Preece (née Williams) **1985**
Hannah Preston **2003**
Clive Prestt **1976**
Giles Rabbitts **2007**
Elizabeth Rae **2006**

Matthew J. Reed **1997**
Martin Riley **1979**
Brendan Roach **2008**
Caroline Kayleigh Roberts **2005**
Julian Robertson-Kellie **1982**
Jim Roe **1972**
The Revd John R. Rowlands **1954**
James Michael Roylance **2005**
Duncan Ruckledge **1990**
Donald J. Rudalevige **1962**
Richard Rule **1977**
The Revd Dr William G. Rusch **1963**
Graham Russell **1972**
Professor Ian Sargent **Fellow 1983–**
Richard Saynor **2004**
Benjamin Schliemann **1987**
Revd Donald Schofield **1949**
Harley G.M. Schumann **2010**
Mark Scott **2008**
Daniel Seiderer **2007**
Philip Charles Selbie
Benjamin Sennitt **1989**
David Seymour **1973**
Gregory J. Shaffer **1969**
Shamit Shah **1983**
Alan Shaw **1987**
Noel L. Shepherd **1956**
Franklin Sherman
Becky Shaw Simms **1996**
Bob Skelly **1965**
Glenton Smith **1992**
Philip Smith **1967**
Richard Smith **1993**
Douglas Charles Stange **1982**
Gavin Steele **1979**
Jonathan M. Steinberg **1988**
Revd Graham Stephenson **1967**
Benjamin Stevens **2006**
Carl R. Stockton **1965**
Charlotte A. Stonehouse **2005**
Tim Storrie **1986**
Martin Stott **1973**
Emma Sullivan **2008**
Richard and Rosalind Swift
Dr D.A. Sykes **1955**
Principal 1977–86
John Sykes **Fellow 1987–2010**
Kuan Ern Tan **1996**
Daniel J. Tarry **2011**
John James Taylor **1992**
Revd Bill Thomas **1985**
Steve Thomas **1978**
Andrew Thompson **1987**
John Thorndyke **1963**
Stephen Thorpe **1975**
Anthony David Tucker **1951**
Richard Underhill **1988**
Sue Unerman **1979**
Paul S. Vine **1981**
Alexander Walford
Dr Diana Walford CBE
Principal 2002–11
M. and G. Wall **1995**
Mike Walton **1956**
Steve Waterman **Bursar 2003–12**
Rob Wellburn **2006**
Nora E. Wetzel **2005**
Hilary White **2010**
Martin Wiggins **1981**
Angela Williams (née Burns) **1981**
Bruce M. Williams **1966**
Chris Williams **1992**
John Willis **1979**
Peter Wilson **1969**
Joanne Woodward **1995**
His Honour Judge
Paul Worsley QC **1966**
Brigitte Worth **1994**
Tom Young **2008**

Index

Page numbers in *italics* refer to illustrations; those in **bold** to contributors

Acknowledgements

The editors gratefully acknowledge the contributions included in this volume from colleagues and former students, and the good will emanating from all corners of the College. Equipped with her camera, Keiko Ikeuchi attended numerous college events, providing a photographic record of Mansfield throughout the year, and we are also indebted to Katherine Blundell for additional photography. Particular thanks are due to Alma Jenner, who scoured the college archive, unearthing, identifying and cataloguing countless images and documents, and generously offering wise comments, to Jane Buswell, Sally Jones and Oliver Mahony for their invaluable assistance in checking facts and sourcing archive images, and to Clare Howell who, together with colleagues at Third Millennium, steered the project to completion, caring deeply about all details as well as the big picture.

Tony Berezny heads the maintenance department, which has worked wonders in preserving the fabric of the College.

Picture Credits

Unless otherwise noted, the illustrations in this book have been provided by Mansfield College Archive. Every effort has been made to identify the photographers correctly and we apologize unreservedly to any copyright holder who has not been duly credited, and will endeavour to do so in any future edition:

Peter Armstrong 29; Katherine Blundell 35, 62L, 70T, 72–3, 74–5, 76, 90–1, 99, 118, 123, 172; Stephen Blundell 92; Paul Crossley 154T; Roy Fox for Mansfield College Archive 126–7; Isabel Franke 141; Guy Hands 42R; Shu-chuen Huang 165BR; Keiko Ikeuchi 4–5, 6, 7, 8–9, 28, 31, 32TB, 36, 40(all), 43B, 44, 46TB, 47, 54–5, 60, 61R, 62–3, 65, 66T, 67, 68–9, 70B, 77, 78, 79, 82, 85, 96, 106–7, 108–9, 125, 128–9, 130–1, 132–3, 134, 138L, 140R, 142–3, 144, 145L, 146–7, 152–3, 155, 156M, 157L, 158, 159, 160–1, 162–3, 164, 165T, 166–9, 177; John Lysons 34, 52; Rick Mather Architects 43T; Prof Mikolaski 22T, 23L; NASA 140; National Portrait Gallery 12, 15R, 58L; Oxford University Press 112B; Rick Pearson 136–7; Susan Pugsley 71B; rob@robjudges.com 48; Alister Thorpe 7; Stephen Turnbull 93; Henry Uniacke 83T, 86T, 101
Front and back jacket: Keiko Ikeuchi

Library
Professors and class rooms
Sc